SECRETS OF THE ZOHAR

The Kabbalah Centre
155 E. 48th St., New York, NY 10017
1062 S. Robertson Blvd., Los Angeles, CA 90035

First Edition February 2007
Second Edition October 2008
Printed in USA
ISBN10: 1-57189-577-9
ISBN13: 978-1-57189-577-6

Design: HL Design (Hyun Min Lee) www.hldesignco.com

SECRETS
OF THE
ZOHAR

STORIES AND MEDITATIONS
TO AWAKEN THE HEART

www.kabbalah.com™

MICHAEL BERG

EDITOR OF THE FIRST COMPLETE
ENGLISH TRANSLATION OF THE ZOHAR

TABLE OF CONTENTS

Foreword   ix

INTRODUCTION   1

Appreciating the Zohar   15

Unconditional Love   20

I. MEDITATIONS FOR LIFE'S CHALLENGES

Finding Strength When You Feel Powerless: 27
   "The son of Rav Yosi of Peki'in"

Overcoming Fear: 37
   "A formidable mountain"

When You Need Protection: 43
   "And the fear of you and the dread of you"

The Power of Forgiveness to Remove Judgment: 47
   "Rav Aba and the traveler"

Finding Light in the Darkness: 52
   "Rav Shimon's departure from the cave"

When You Need to Remove Envy and Jealousy: 58
   "Do not eat the bread of one who has an evil eye"

Understanding the Opponent, the Source of All Chaos   62
and Negativity:
   "With all your heart, and with all your soul, and
   with all your might"

Connecting to Your Soul Mate   68

Starting Something New: 73
   "Bringing in the Light"

Replacing Doubt with Certainty: 77
   "Her husband is known in the gates"

Desiring More, and Not Settling for Less: 82
   "The Concealed Book"

Drawing in Miracles: 87
   "The wife of Obadiah"

Transforming Grief: 91
   "The passing of the three friends"

II. MEDITATIONS FOR SPIRITUAL GROWTH

Wholehearted Effort and Infinite Reward: 101
   "They should bring me an offering"

When You Want to Turn Back Time: 106
   "This is the book of the generations of Adam"

Awakening Desire for the Light: 111
   "He did neither eat bread nor drink water"

Giving Power to Your Prayers   115

Awakening Your Desire to Fulfill Your Potential: 119
   "When Rav Shimon wanted to depart from the world"

When There's Too Much to Do and You're Feeling Overwhelmed: 125
   "The importance of small openings"

Erasing the Ego: 129
   "He who is small is great"

Having Certainty in the Spiritual System,   133
Even When the Outcome Is in Doubt

Preparation   139

III. Meditations for Greater Awareness

Expanding Your Yearning for the Light: 147
"The vision of Rav Chiya"

When You Need to Remove Judgments From Your Life: 152
"Rav Yitzchak and the power of change"

A Place Beyond Death: 162
"The channel of immortality"

Assistance From the Souls of the Righteous: 168
"The passing of Rav Shimon"

The Source of All True Fulfillment: 173
"Rav Aba and Rav Yosi"

Becoming Balanced: 180
"The foreword to the Idra Raba"

Understanding the Greater Reality: 183
"Removing the fear of death"

Spiritual Teachers and Friends: 187
"Whose heart is awakened"

The Battle: 192
"The Opponent is attacking"

Helping Others: 198
"Pursue those who have not overcome their negative inclination"

Spreading the Zohar: 203
"When the Zohar will be revealed, multitudes will gather to it"

Tree of Life: 206
"Because they will taste the Zohar"

Immortality: 209
"He will swallow up death forever"

FOREWORD

In September of 2004, my father had a stroke.

At the time, the doctors were not sure if he would live or die, and their outlook as to his quality of life, if he did survive, was bleak.

Since then my father has made an amazing recovery, although he is not the same person he was before the stroke. Those of us who are close to him have different understandings of why this had to happen and why he has changed.

Today, he has little if any desire to teach or write; mostly, he wants to pray.

I have been learning from him in my dreams.

A few months ago as I started working on this book, I had a dream my father was talking to me about the Zohar. As time passes, I have become fuzzy about the details but not the message. My father said, "I have been saying it for years, but nobody has heard, 'its all about the Zohar'"

The "it" he referred to in my dream is the great work he and my mother have been a part of for more than forty years, the work that began at the creation of this world: to bring about the perfected world where there will be peace and fulfillment for all. The kabbalists teach this will be achieved when a critical mass of light is revealed in our world through the positive actions of humanity.

What he said in the dream was no different than what he had said a thousand times before. The most important instrument we have to bring about this amazing global transformation is the Zohar.

Only after his stroke and this dream did I begin to truly understand his simple message. It is my hope that I continue to hear him and *do* what ever I can to make the Zohar available to all.

It is my honor to write this book as another step in the process of bringing all of us closer to a world with no more pain, no more suffering, and even as the Bible and the Zohar promise, a world with no death.

I dedicate this book to my father, Rav Berg; may he have complete and total recovery and may he merit to see his vision of a chaos-free world manifest in his lifetime. And also to my mother, Karen, without whose strength, unwavering commitment, and gentle prodding none of this work could have been accomplished. Who still, through her pain, continues to push forward their dream, a dream they carried from the great kabbalists of the past thousands of years.

I pray for myself and for all of us to remember: "It is all about the Zohar."

With tears, love, light, and certainty,

Michael Berg, Los Angeles, CA, February 2007

Introduction

Before time, before space, before a single atom came into being, the thought of creation was already a reality in the mind of God. This thought was, and is, the vision of a perfect world—without pain, without suffering, without death—bringing unlimited abundance and fulfillment to every soul.

This perfect world is much more than a mere vision. It is a reality. It exists. It is a parallel universe right here, right now, concealed only until we achieve our purpose in this world.

Why is the perfect world concealed? Because nothing can be given to us unearned. We have come into this world in search of the Light—but the Light is already here, if only we can make ourselves ready to receive it.

That is our purpose. To help us achieve it, God has given us the supremely powerful instrument known as the Zohar.

As you begin your study and exploration of the Zohar, it's important to understand what "the thought of creation" really means. Before the creation of this physical world, a vision existed in the mind of God, a vision of a perfect world, free from all pain and suffering, with joy and fulfillment for everyone. But the divine thought of creation is much more than a mere vision. Because the Creator is not limited by time or space, the perfected world already exists. That world, where all pain and suffering are removed, is a reality at this moment.

As the kabbalists teach, however, entrance to that world cannot simply be given to us. We must earn it and achieve it through our spiritual work and transformation. To make this possible, the Creator has given us a great gift—a portal into the perfect world. That portal is the Zohar, the most powerful tool for our transformation. As our hearts awaken to the Zohar, we literally step through a splendid gateway into the perfect world and bring it into our lives. The more we connect to the Zohar, the more our world merges with the Creator's vision. To advance this process, many translations of the Zohar and other kabbalistic writings have been completed over the centuries. As great as these accomplishments have been, however, they have not been accessible to everyone. This book takes the next step: it extends an invitation to the Zohar for anyone who wishes to enter.

The truth is, each of us already has a connection to the supernal reality. Your perfected self already exists in the thought of Creation. As you study the Zohar, as your eyes pass over its Aramaic letters, and as you meditate on its teachings, you begin to reveal your perfect self in this world. Moreover, Kabbalah teaches that as greater and greater numbers of people also begin this study, we will achieve the ultimate transformation of the physical world.

Physically, the Zohar is a book, or more often a set of books, but its physical form is actually a source of great misunderstanding. Its content provides commentary on the Bible in the form of conversations among spiritual masters, but the greatest sages of Kabbalah teach that just as the Zohar's contents embody the Light of the Creator so do the very words and letters themselves. The fact that the Zohar is given to us in the *form* of a book is part of a strategy to make it accessible to every person on earth.

As our connection with the Zohar grows deeper, so does our connection to the Creator's Light. For those who approach the Zohar with sincerity and an open heart, it is the greatest gift that can be received or given. And as Rav Shimon bar Yochai explains in the Zohar's pages; only by bringing the Light of the

Zohar to the world that the perfected world will be achieved—
a world set free from pain, suffering, and death. This is the reason that the kabbalists were so passionately committed to
revealing the Zohar.

Reading the Zohar: Awakening the Light

The experience of reading an ordinary book or article is exactly what it seems: We're just *reading*. But studying and reading
the Zohar actually awakens the very energies we're reading
about. When we study a passage concerning mercy, for example, that aspect of the Creator's Light is awakened in ourselves
and even in the world as a whole. We become more merciful,
more forgiving, which in turn elicits the quality of mercy from
others. When we scan the Zohar's passages dealing with judgment, we gain the power to remove judgments placed upon us,
while also erasing our own judgmental tendencies.

Imagine this: You meet a friend for lunch, and she shows you
an old photo. It's a picture of a husband and wife, obviously
taken in a foreign land many years ago. At first, you might be
mildly interested in the picture, but the strange clothes, the poor
lighting, and your lack of connection to the two people would
make it difficult for you to be deeply moved by the photo.

Just to be polite, you might compliment your friend on the
antique she's found, and then hand the picture back to her.

"But wait!" she might say. "Aren't you totally enthralled by this
photograph? Don't you feel a huge surge of emotion when you
look at it?"

"Well, no," you'd reply, trying to be patient with your friend.
"Why should I feel anything about it at all? I don't know these

two people, so I can't relate to them. I don't know where the picture was taken, so I don't feel connected to it. I really don't know anything about what's happening in this picture. Why should I care about it?"

"Well, suppose I told you that someone devoted a lot of time and effort to finding this photo for you. You see, the people in the picture are your great-great-grandparents, who lived more than a hundred years ago."

If you were to hear this information, there's no doubt that your whole attitude toward the picture would instantly change. It would be the same photo as before, but it would suddenly become amazingly interesting. You'd look at the people in the photo in a whole new way. You'd try to find any slight resemblance to yourself or to your parents. You'd wonder where these people had lived, how they'd met, how they'd made their living, and perhaps how they'd died.

Above and beyond questions like this, you would undoubtedly have a strong emotional reaction to the picture. Powerful feelings would suddenly be ignited in your heart, perhaps unlike any you'd ever had before. For the rest of your life, you would always remember this picture and the circumstances under which you first saw it. Yet just a moment earlier, it would have seemed utterly forgettable. There would have appeared to have been no reason to get excited about it.

For most people, the Zohar is much like the photograph I've just described. At first, it can seem remote and even forbidding in its strangeness and complexity. But the purpose of this book is to let you know, simply and directly, that at the deepest level of your soul, there is a profound connection between the Zohar and who you are.

The more you study the Zohar, the better you will grasp what this means. But right now, even if you don't completely understand it, I hope you will let yourself experience the connection with the Zohar that already exists within you. Open yourself to this power, and it will be there for you.

God's Light is like a bottomless well, unlimited in the amount of water it can provide. Our consciousness is like a vessel, a receiving entity that is also boundless. The larger this vessel becomes, the more water we can draw from the well. The higher our level of consciousness, the more Light we receive. Our task is to open ourselves more and more to the Light by expanding the volume of our spiritual vessel.

Toward this end, studying and meditating upon the pages of the Zohar is vitally important. What's more, this should be done not only in translation but in the original language, as well, even if you don't "understand" a single word. For this reason, both the original Aramaic text of the Zohar passages as well as the English translation have been included in this book. Since the kabbalists teach that simply having the Zohar in your home brings connection with the Creator's Light, reading, meditating, or scanning the pages can be even more powerful—even if you encounter something outside your comprehension. Once again, the reason for this lies in the fact that the Zohar is much more than just a book of wisdom. The Zohar is an energy source. It's a means of accessing the divine Light that resides in the soul of every human being. Any connection with the Zohar brings Light. The deeper your connection, the greater the revelation of Light will be.

The Zohar's History

The Zohar has existed forever, although not in its present form as a book. The Zohar began as an oral tradition of secrets. Adam possessed the Zohar, as did the patriarchs of the Bible. At Mount Sinai, Moses received the Torah (that is, spiritual wisdom) and also the secrets of the Zohar in spoken form. These were passed from one generation to the next, but they were not written down until Rav Shimon bar Yochai was granted divine permission to give the ancient secrets in written form.

The Zohar was originally composed in Aramaic, a language widely spoken in the ancient world but now largely forgotten. It was first written down approximately two thousand years ago, although the exact date is uncertain. But more than being written, the Zohar was *revealed*.

Although secular scholars have disagreed about the Zohar's authorship, from a spiritual perspective this is a meaningless debate. Once we appreciate the greatness of the Zohar's wisdom, it becomes clear that the author—whoever this may have been—was a truly exalted soul. Still, whenever the Zohar's authorship has been discussed by kabbalists throughout history, it has been agreed that the author must have been Rav Shimon bar Yochai. No lesser soul could have been a channel for this revelation. As Rav Yehuda Ashlag, the great twentieth-century kabbalist, expressed it: "From the day that I have been enabled, by means of the Light of the Almighty, to peruse this holy book, it never entered my mind to investigate its authorship. The reason for this is simple. The contents of the book caused my mind to conjure up the cherished excellence of the authority of Rav Shimon bar Yochai incalculably more than any of the other holy masters."

During Rav Shimon's lifetime, the text of the Zohar was written down by his student, Rabbi Abba. But, in the centuries that followed, and as the Zohar itself had predicted, the Zohar was largely hidden from the world. The sages of Kabbalah realized that the revelation of the Zohar must await the day when humanity as a whole was ready to receive it. The Zohar re-emerged in the thirteenth century through the efforts of Rav Moses deLeon, in Spain. But it was not until 1540 that a prominent kabbalist of the era, Rav Abraham Azulai, declared that the time had come for the Zohar to be disseminated to all of humanity. "From now on," he wrote, "the basic levels of Kabbalah must be taught to everyone young and old. Only through Kabbalah will we forever eliminate war, destruction, and man's inhumanity to his fellow man." Rav Azulai invoked passages in the Zohar depicting a future in which even small children would come to know the teachings of Kabbalah.

The next great development in kabbalistic revelation came from Rav Isaac Luria, known as the Ari, who was born in Jerusalem in 1534. After moving from Jerusalem to Egypt as a young man, he adopted the existence of a hermit scholar, isolating himself with the Zohar in a cottage by the Nile. According to Kabbalah, Elijah the Prophet and a whole host of angels joined him in his study, and there Rav Luria attained a supremely powerful connection to the Light of the Creator.

At age thirty-six, the Ari was told by Elijah to go to the Holy Land, to the town of Safed, a spiritual community located in what is now Israel. There he was to meet a scholar, Chaim Vital, and instruct him.

At that time, Rav Vital was struggling with a challenging section of the Zohar. He had spent weeks praying, meditating, begging for the revelation of the wisdom, trying to decipher its code. At the time, Rav Luria was earning his living as a humble shopkeeper. After they met, Rav Vital asked himself, *How can I learn spiritual wisdom from a man who does nothing but work in a shop?* Then he began to have a recurring dream. In the dream, Rav Luria was effortlessly explaining the Zohar to him.

Compelled by the power of this dream, Rav Vital sought out Rav Luria, but again his doubt overcame him. As Rav Vital turned to leave, Rav Luria asked him if he was familiar with a certain section of the Zohar. Rav Vital turned in astonishment; it was precisely the passage with which he was struggling.

Rav Luria did indeed open up the wisdom of the text to him, and once the Light contained in that passage was revealed to Rav Vital, he knew Rav Luria was meant to be his teacher from that moment on. Like Rav Shimon bar Yochai, Rav Luria never wrote a word. His wisdom was passed orally to his students, who recorded his teachings.

Christian Kabbalists

Although some believe that the Zohar is a Jewish text meant only for select scholars, the Zohar has always been studied by all people. During the fifteenth century, for example, there was a significant movement of Christian Kabbalists across Europe.

One of the first Christian scholars of Kabbalah was Giovanni Pico della Mirandola, an intellectual prodigy and renowned Italian humanist. Pico saw Kabbalah as an unbroken oral tradition extending back to Moses on Mount Sinai. He considered the Zohar a divine revelation, the lost key to understanding ancient teachings that were capable of unraveling the inner secrets of Christianity.

Pico died at the age of thirty-one. His efforts to disseminate Kabbalah to the Christian world were carried on by Johannes Reuchlin, a pioneer in the study of the Hebrew language. Like Pico, in his book *On the Art of the Kabbalah*, Reuchlin argued that Christian teachings could not be truly understood without an understanding of kabbalistic principles. A further development occurred in the seventeenth century, when the Kabbalists Christian Knorr von Rosenroth and Francis von Helmont produced a Latin translation of the Zohar. This text, known as the *Kabbalah Denudata*, influenced many great scholars and scientists of the time, including Gottfried Leibniz in Germany and Sir Isaac Newton in England. Newton's copy of the Zohar in Latin can be seen today in the library of Cambridge University.

Reading the Zohar

Once opened, the door to the Zohar has never closed. Spiritual and intellectual giants throughout history have turned to the Zohar to unravel the mysteries of the universe—and Rav Isaac Luria predicted that a day will come when the Zohar will be available to "every man, woman and child." This new era began with the work of Rav Yehuda Ashlag, who founded the organization now known as The Kabbalah Centre. Rav Ashlag is responsible for the first unabridged translation of the Zohar from the original Aramaic into Hebrew. When Rav Ashlag passed on, his student Rav Yehuda Brandwein took on the work of disseminating the wisdom of the Zohar, and after Rav Brandwein's passing in 1969, Rav Berg and Karen Berg continued that process. Their work led to a historic turning point in the process of making the Zohar accessible to all humanity: the first English translation of the entire Zohar, with Rav Ashlag's commentary, which was published by The Kabbalah Centre in 1995. I was blessed to be the editor of this work, which required ten years and the collective efforts of dozens of people. As a result, the Zohar is now available to the vast international community of English speakers.

The Zohar's Language and Letters

The Zohar is written in the ancient language of Aramaic, a sister language to Hebrew that employs Hebrew letters. While Hebrew was the language of the upper classes, Aramaic was the language of the common people. The Zohar's revelation in Aramaic is a message that this tool of Light can and should be used by all people, regardless of their spiritual level.

In our everyday lives, we're used to thinking of the letters of the English alphabet in purely functional terms. The letters are units we put together to create words, just as bricks are the units we use to create a wall. We think of both the letters and the bricks in practical rather than spiritual terms: They're small, inert objects we use to create larger objects.

The letters of the Hebrew alphabet (used for both Aramaic and Hebrew) should be understood in an entirely different way. In addition to its functional importance as the component of a word, each Hebrew letter is also a channel of spiritual energy—and this is true whether or not we know what the letter sounds like or how it fits into a given word. The more we know about the combination and sequence of letters, the richer our connection through them becomes. As the kabbalists make clear, the Hebrew alphabet, the Hebrew language, and the Aramaic language, as well, are universal tools intended for all humankind. The ultimate purpose of these tools is spiritual connection.

Likewise, the Zohar itself is a divine gift to everyone, not just to one nation or religion. The Hebrew alphabet is a tool given to all humankind by the Creator. Focused concentration on the Hebrew letters is a powerful form of kabbalistic meditation. Just letting your eyes pass over the letters opens a channel to the Light. This is something anyone *can* do, and it's something everyone *should* do to make best use of the Creator's gift.

As You Begin . . .

Rav Ashlag's translation and commentary on the Zohar is entitled *Ha Sulam*, or *The Ladder*. As Rav Ashlag explained:

> *I called this commentary 'The Ladder' to demonstrate that the function of my commentary is the same as that of a ladder. When there is a high-level room, full of all manner of good things, all that is needed is a ladder to climb up to it and then all the goodness of the world will be within one's reach. However, a ladder serves no end in itself. That is to say, if one should simply rest upon a rung of the ladder and not enter into the room, one's intentions will not be fulfilled.*
>
> *The same is true of my commentary on the Zohar. The words have not yet been invented that completely convey the deep meanings of the text. So what I have done is to provide a path and an introduction for any person who should wish, by means of it, to delve into the holy Zohar itself. Only then will my intention have been achieved.*

Just as Rav Ashlag described his work as a ladder, I hope this book will also serve as a ladder for this generation to connect with the amazing Light that is the Zohar.

Secrets of the Zohar: Format and Foundations

The organization of this book is very straightforward. Selections from the Zohar have been carefully organized to provide a system for study and meditation. A brief introductory section precedes each selection to explain the passage and its power in our daily lives; this is followed by a meditation for putting that power into action. Just as studying the Zohar brings connection to the Light, so does meditating on the original words and letters. Therefore, the Aramaic text of each selection is also provided.

I've chosen two sections of the Zohar to begin this book, as a way of introducing the organization and format of what will follow. The first introductory section is the story of how the power and importance of the Zohar was revealed, and the gathering together of many righteous souls to assist in this great revelation. The second introductory passage deals with an important kabbalistic aspect of love and the fact that the Zohar's Light could be revealed only through the love that existed among the friends surrounding Rav Shimon bar Yochai. It is my hope that these two introductory sections will open your heart and path to the Light of the Zohar.

APPRECIATING THE ZOHAR

(HAKDAMAT, TIKUNEI ZOHAR, VERSE 1)

Often in life, we may miss out on great gifts. We don't make the most of the great blessings that are available to us because we don't appreciate what has been given. Kabbalah teaches that to gain the benefit of the gifts that are intended for us, we need to have appreciation for them. This is also true for the spiritual tools we have been given, and especially for the Zohar. To maximize the connection to the Light that takes place when we study passages from the Zohar, including those in this book, we should nurture our appreciation for what the Zohar is and for how it was created. As the Zohar itself tells us, its secrets were meant to be concealed until our generation, which is called the generation of *Mashiach* (Messiah). This does not refer to a person, but to a level of global consciousness that is achieved by all humankind.

The revelation of the Zohar was the physical expression of the thought of Creation: the total and complete Light of fulfillment. The Zohar's revelation was an absolutely unique, hugely significant event, comparable only to the revelation of the Bible at Mount Sinai. Never before—and certainly never since—have all the souls of the righteous and all the sacred names assisted in such a historical process. The Zohar is the greatest treasury of Light ever received by humankind. Thanks to the Zohar at every moment, we can discover and connect with more and more of that Light. This is not just an amazing opportunity. It is nothing less than the true purpose of our lives.

This passage is the beginning of a portion of the Zohar known as the *Tikunei Zohar* ("the corrections of the Zohar"). It consists of seventy explanations of *Beresheet*, the first word of the Torah. Rav Shimon bar Yochai revealed these secrets during the twelve years he spent in a cave, hidden from the Romans. During those years, the Creator and all the great souls of history came into his presence.

Rav Shimon ran away to the desert of Lod and hid in a cave — he and his son Rav Elazar. A miracle occurred for them: a carob tree sprouted and a new spring of water appeared. They ate from the carob tree and drank from the spring. Eliyahu would come to them twice every day, and study with them, and no one knew where they were.

1. רַבִּי שִׁמְעוֹן אָזַל לֵיהּ וְעָרַק לְמַדְבְּרָא דְּלוֹד וְאִתְגְּנִיז בְּחַד מְעַרְתָּא, הוּא וְרַבִּי אֶלְעָזָר בְּרֵיהּ אִתְרְחִישׁ נִיסָא, נָפַק לְהוֹן חַד חֲרוּב, וְחַד מַעֲיָינָא דְּמַיָּא, אָכְלֵי מֵהַהוּא חֲרוּב, וְשָׁתָן מֵהַהוּא מַיָּא, הֲוָה אֵלִיָּהוּ זָכוּר לַטּוֹב אָתֵי לְהוֹן בְּכָל יוֹמָא תְּרֵי זִמְנֵי, וְאוֹלִיף לוֹן וְלָא יְדַע אִינִישׁ בְּהוֹ כו׳.

Arise, Rav Shimon, and begin speaking before the *Shechinah*. He began and said, "And the wise shall shine like the brightness (Zohar) of the firmament."

2. קוּם רַבִּי שִׁמְעוֹן אַפְתַּח מִלִּין קָמֵי שְׁכִינְתָּא. פָּתַח וְאָמַר וְהַמַּשְׂכִּילִים יַזְהִירוּ כְּזֹהַר הָרָקִיעַ וגו׳.

The "wise" referred to in the verse, are Rav Shimon and his friends. "Shall shine" means that when they came together to reveal the Zohar, they were given permission from above. Permission was also granted to Eliyahu and to all the souls in the supernal academy to come down to them, and also to the angels that are concealed, and to the angels that are in the way of understanding.

3. וְהַמַּשְׂכִּילִים אִלֵּין רַבִּי שִׁמְעוֹן וְחַבְרַיָּיא. יַזְהִירוּ, כַּד אִתְכַּנָּשׁוּ לְמֶעֱבַד הַאי חִבּוּרָא, רְשׁוּתָא אִתְיְהִיב לְהוֹן וּלְאֵלִיָּהוּ עִמְּהוֹן, וּלְכָל נִשְׁמָתִין דִּמְתִיבְתָּאן לְנַחֲתָא בֵּינַיְיהוּ, וּלְכָל מַלְאֲכַיָּא בְּאִתְכַּסְיָא, וּבְאָרַח שֵׂכֶל.

And the Cause of all Causes gave permission to all the holy names, to all the combinations of the Tetragrammaton, and to all the other appellations, to reveal to them concealed secrets—every name on its level. And He gave permission to the ten *Sefirot* to reveal to them concealed secrets, that these secrets were not permitted to be revealed until the time of the generation of *Mashiach* (Messiah).

4. וְעִלַּת עַל כֹּלָּא יְהִיב רְשׁוּ לְכָל שְׁמָהָן קַדִּישִׁין, וּלְכָל הֲוָיָין וּלְכָל כִּנּוּיִין, לְגַלָּאָה לוֹן רָזִין טְמִירִין, כָּל שֵׁם בְּדַרְגָּא דִּילֵיהּ. וּרְשׁוּתָא יְהִיב לַעֲשַׂר סְפִירָן לְגַלָּאָה לוֹן רָזִין טְמִירִין, דְּלָא אִתְיְהִיב רְשׁוּ לְגַלָּאָה לוֹן עַד דְּיֵיתֵי דָרָא דְמַלְכָּא מְשִׁיחָא.

MEDITATION

This meditation awakens our appreciation of the source and the power of the Zohar, and allows us to access that power. It also brings us connection with the great souls who assisted Rav Shimon bar Yochai in the revelation of the Zohar. As we study the Zohar, we should always be aware of its great power and the unity of souls that came together for its revelation. The greater our appreciation for this immense gift, the more of the Zohar's Light we can reveal.

← reading and scanning direction

וְהַמַשְׂכִּילִים אֵלִין רַבִּי שִׁמְעוֹן וְחַבְרַיָּיא.
vechavraya Shimon Rabbi ilein vehamaskilim

יַזְהִירוּ, כַּד אִתְכַּנְשׁוּ לְמֶעֱבַד הַאי חִבּוּרָא,
chibura hay leme'evad itkanshu kad yazhiru

רְשׁוּתָא אִתְיְהִיב לְהוֹן וּלְאֵלִיָּהוּ עִמְּהוֹן,
imhon ule'Eliyahu lehon ityahiv reshuta

וּלְכָל נִשְׁמָתִין דִּמְתִיבְתָּאן לְנַחֲתָא בֵּינַיְיהוּ,
beinayehu lenachata dimtivtaan nishmatin ulechol

וּלְכָל מַלְאָכַיָּא בְּאִתְכַּסְיָא, וּבְאָרַח שֵׂכֶל.
sechel uvorach be'itkasya mal'achaya ulechol

The "wise" referred to in the verse, are Rav Shimon and his friends. "Shall shine" means that when they came together to reveal the Zohar, they were given permission from above. Permission was also granted to Elijah and to all the souls in the supernal academy to come down to them, and also to the angels that are concealed, and to the angels that are in the way of understanding.

UNCONDITIONAL LOVE

(ZOHAR, KI TISA, VERSE 54)

One of Kabbalah's most important teachings is that, to be successful, any endeavor must have unity among everyone involved. Certainly this was true for the revelation of the Zohar. In this section, the Zohar itself describes the unique reality that enabled its great revelation in the time of Rav Shimon bar Yochai. Surprisingly, the essence of that reality was not great learning or righteousness, but the unconditional, endless love that was present among the friends, as the students of Rav Shimon were called.

To bring the greatest possible Light into our lives through our study of the Zohar, we too should grow our capacity for unconditional love. This is what enabled Rav Shimon's great revelations, and this is what we need in order to reveal the Light for ourselves.

For Rav Aba said, "All the friends who do not love each other die before their time." All the friends during the days of Rav Shimon loved each other, soul and spirit. Therefore, in the generation of Rav Shimon the secrets of the Torah were unveiled. For Rav Shimon used to say: "All the friends that do not love each other cause themselves to deviate from the straight path. Also, they blemish the spiritual wisdom, because the wisdom has in it love, friendship and truth. Abraham loved Yitzchak and Yitzchak loved Abraham, so they embraced each other. Both were attached to Yaakov with love and friendship, and gave their spirit to each other. The friends must be like them, and not cause a blemish in them."

54. דְּאָמַר רְבִּי אַבָּא, כָּל אִלֵּין וַזַבְרַיָּיא, דְּלָא רְחִימִין אִלֵּין לְאִלֵּין, אִסְתָּלָקוּ מֵעָלְמָא עַד לָא מָטָא זִמְנַיְיהוּ, כֹּל וַזַבְרַיָּיא בְּיוֹמוֹי דְּר"ש, רְחִימוּ דְּנַפְשָׁא וְרוּחָא הֲוָה בֵּינַיְיהוּ, וּבְג'כ בְּדָרָא דְּר' שִׁמְעוֹן בְּאִתְגַּלְיָיא הֲוָה, דַּהֲוָה אָמַר רְבִּי שִׁמְעוֹן, כָּל וַזַבְרַיָּיא דְּלָא רְחִימִין אִלֵּין לְאִלֵּין, גַּרְמִין דְּלָא לְיֵיהַךְ בְּאֹרַח מֵישָׁר. וְעוֹד דְּעַבְדִּין פְּגִימוּ בָּהּ, דְּהָא אוֹרַיְיתָא רְחִימוּ וְאַחְוָה וּקְשׁוֹט אִית בָּהּ. אַבְרָהָם רָחִים לְיִצְחָק, יִצְחָק לְאַבְרָהָם, מִתְחַבְּקָן דָּא בְּדָא, יַעֲקֹב תַּרְוַויְיהוּ אֲחִידָן בֵּיהּ, בִּרְחִימוּ, וּבְאַחְוָה, יָהֲבִין רוּחַיְיהוּ דָּא בְּדָא. וַזַבְרַיָּיא כְּהַהוּא דּוּגְמָא אִצְטְרִיכוּ, וְלָא לְמֶעְבַּד פְּגִימוּ.

MEDITATION

Growing our capacity to love others is essential for our own growth. This meditation brings awareness of the importance of unconditional love and helps us to awaken that love in ourselves.

כֹּל חַבְרַיָּיא בְּיוֹמוֹי דְּר'ש, רְחִימוּ
kol chavraya beyomoi de Ribbi Shimon rechimu

דְּנַפְשָׁא וְרוּחָא הֲוָה בֵּינַיְיהוּ, ובג"כ
denafsha verucha hava beinayehu uveginkach

בְּדָרָא דְּר שִׁמְעוֹן בְּאִתְגַּלְיָיא הֲוָה
bedara deRibbi Shimon be'itgalya hava

All the friends during the days of Rav Shimon loved each other, soul and spirit. Therefore, in the generation of Rav Shimon the secrets of the Torah were unveiled.

I
Meditations
for Life's
Challenges

FINDING STRENGTH WHEN YOU
FEEL POWERLESS:

"THE SON OF RAV YOSI OF PEKI'IN"

(ZOHAR, BALAK, VERSE 357)

There are times when our problems seem stronger than our ability to deal with them. Actually, that feeling of powerlessness is itself one of the most destructive tools of the negative side. It's also an illusion. Each of us has within us a part of the Creator, which is the soul, and which gives us the power to accomplish much more than we might ever imagine. But to make use of our power, we first need to be aware of its presence within us, even at the moments when we feel weak, small, and most incapable of change.

This section of the Zohar tells of how even a small child had the ability to bring about his father's resurrection from death, inspiring us to realize that no matter how small we may be, nothing is too big for us when we are connected with the Light. The section begins with Rav Elazar traveling with Rav Aba and several of the other friends to visit Rav Elazar's father-in-law, Rav Yosi, who is ill. They have received a message that Rav Yosi will not die, but that a different Rav Yosi—Rav Yosi of Peki'in—will die in his place.

Rav Elazar and Rav Aba visit the house of Rav Yosi of Peki'in, who has died. They find Rav Yosi of Peki'in's small son in terrible grief. He won't allow anyone else near the body. The boy declares to God that God should not have taken his father. Instead, God should have taken the boy and his sister. At that moment, a supernal voice declares that Rav Yosi of Peki'in has been given another twenty-two years of life. Thirteen other people, whose time had come to die, have been taken in his place. Now Rav Yosi of Peki'in will have time to instruct his son in his studies. Rav Yosi of Peki'in is returned to life amid much rejoicing. He describes what took place when he was in the Upper World, and how his son's offering to give up his own life led to God's mercy.

We are in this world to do our spiritual work, and to help others complete theirs. Rav Yosi of Peki'in had completed his work. He did not need to live on for himself. But because his son still needed his instruction, Rav Yosi of Peki'in was given twenty-two more years. This is a very important lesson. Helping others to grow is not just an opportunity. It is a fundamental reason why we remain in this world. Specifically, the teaching of a child is extremely important, as it written: "The world is sustained by the breath of the spiritual study of young children."

As they were traveling, a dove approached Rav Elazar, chirping and landing before him. Rav Elazar declared, "Worthy dove, you are always faithful in your mission. Go and inform Rav Yosi, my father-in-law, to be prepared for the friends that are coming, and tell him I am with them. A miracle will occur for him in three days. He should have no fear, because we are coming to him in joy." Rav Elazar spoke again, saying, "I am not very happy, for I am greatly disturbed that one full pomegranate (a righteous soul) was given in his stead; his name is also Yosi." The dove left their presence and the friends departed.

357. עַד דַּהֲווֹ אָזְלֵי, הָא יוֹנָה חַד מָטָא לְגַבֵּי רִבִּי אֶלְעָזָר. שְׁרִיאַת, וְקָא מְצַפְצְפָא קַמֵּיהּ. אָמַר רִבִּי אֶלְעָזָר, יוֹנָה כְּשֵׁרָה מְהֵימְנָת הֲוֵית תָּדִיר בִּשְׁלִיחוּתָיךְ, זִילִי וְאֵימָא לֵיהּ, הָא חַבְרַיָּיא אָתָאן לְגַבָּךְ, וַאֲנָא עִמְּהוֹן. וְנִסָּא יִתְרְחִישׁ לֵיהּ לִתְלָתָא יוֹמִין, וְלָא יִדְחַל עֲלֵיהּ דְּוַחֵילוּ, דְּהָא בְּחֶדְוָה אֲנַן אָזְלִין לְגַבֵּיהּ. אָתִיב זִמְנָא אַחֲרָא וְאָמַר, לָא חַדֵּינָא סַגְיָא, וּבָאִישׁ בְּעֵינַי סַגִּי, עַל חַד רִמּוֹנָא מַלְיָא דְּאִתְיְהִיב תְּווֹתֵיהּ, וְיוֹסֵי שְׁמֵיהּ. אָזְלַת הַהִיא יוֹנָה מִקַּמֵּיהּ, וְאִינּוּן חַבְרַיָּיא אָזְלוּ.

Rav Aba said, "Rav Elazar, what is this great wonder that I have observed?" Rav Elazar replied, "This dove came to me on a mission from Rav Yosi, my father-in-law, who is ill. I learned from the dove that he is already saved, that a substitute was given in his stead, and he got well."

358. אָמַר רִבִּי אַבָּא לְרִבִּי אֶלְעָזָר, מַאי הַאי, תַּוְוהָנָא סַגִּי, מִמָּה דַּחֲמֵינָא. אָ"ל, יוֹנָה דָא אָתַאת לְגַבַּאי בִּשְׁלִיחוּתֵיהּ דְּרִבִּי יוֹסֵי חָמִי, דְּאִיהוּ בְּבֵי מַרְעֵיהּ, וְיָדַעְנָא מֵהַאי יוֹנָה דְּאִשְׁתְּזִיב, וְחִלּוּפָא אִתְיְהִיב עֲלֵיהּ וְאִתַּסֵי.

29

As they continued on, behold, a raven appeared to them, crying out and cawing loudly. Rav Elazar said to the raven, "This is your duty, and for this reason you were created. Go on your way, for I already know your news (that the other Rav Yosi is going to die.)" Rav Elazar said, "Let us go and pay our respects for that pomegranate that was full of everything; Rav Yosi of Peki'in was his name. He departed from this world. No one is there who is worthy to take care of him, and he is close by."

359. עַד דַּהֲווֹ אָזְלֵי, הָא עוֹרְבָא חַד קָאִים לְקַמַּיְיהוּ, קָרָא בְּחֵילָא, וּמְצַפְצְפָא צִפְצוּפָא סַגִּי. אָמַר רִבִּי אֶלְעָזָר, לְהָכִי אַתְּ קַיְימָא, וּלְהָכִי אִנְּתְּ מִתַּקָּן, זִיל לְאָרְחָךְ, דְּהָא יְדַעְנָא, אָמַר ר' אֶלְעָזָר, וַתַבְרַיָּיא נֵיזִיל וְנִגְמוֹל חֶסֶד לְרִמּוֹנָא, דַּהֲוָה מַלְיָא מִכֹּלָּא, וְרִבִּי יוֹסֵי דִּפְקִיעִין שְׁמֵיהּ אִיהוּ, דְּהָא אִסְתַּלָּק מֵעָלְמָא דֵּין, וְלֵית מַאן דְּיִזְוֵי לְאִשְׁתַּדְּלָא בֵּיהּ, וְאִיהוּ קָרִיב לְגַבָּן.

They detoured from the road and went to Rav Yosi of Peki'in's house. When the townspeople saw them, they all went to welcome them, and the friends entered the house. Rav Yosi had a little boy who wouldn't allow anyone to get close to the bed of his father after he died. He alone was by it, crying over his father with his mouth over his father's mouth.

360. סָטוּ מֵאָרְחָא, וְאָזְלוּ לְתַמָּן. כֵּיוָן דְּיָזְמוּ לוֹן כָּל בְּנֵי מָאתָא, נַפְקוּ לְגַבַּיְיהוּ. וְעָאלוּ תַּמָּן בְּבֵי רִבִּי יוֹסֵי דִּפְקִיעִין, אִינּוּן וַתַבְרַיָּיא אֲלֵין. בְּרָא זְעֵירָא הֲוָה לֵיהּ לְרִבִּי יוֹסֵי, וְלָא שָׁבִיק לְבַר נָשׁ דְּיִמְטֵי לְעַרְסָא דַּאֲבוּי, בָּתַר דְּמִית. אֶלָּא הֲוָא בִּלְחוֹדוֹי הֲוָה סָמִיךְ לֵיהּ, וּבָכֵי עֲלֵיהּ, פּוּמֵיהּ בְּפוּמֵיהּ מִתְדַּבְּקָא.

The child began and said,

361. פָּתַח הַהוּא יַנּוּקָא וְאָמַר,

"Master of the world, the Torah says: 'If by chance you happen upon a bird's nest... you shall surely let the mother go...'" The child was weeping. He said, "Master of the world, abide by what is written in your Torah. We were two children to my father and mother, myself and my younger sister. You should have taken us, and acted in accordance with the words of the Torah, as is written: 'You shall surely let the mother go, and take the young to you.' Master of the World, if you disagree, for the Torah says 'mother' and not 'father,' know that everything has happened here. For my mother died, and you have taken her away from her children, and now my father also, who protected us, you have taken from his children. Where is the justice of the Torah?" Rav Elazar and his friends wept as they witnessed the grief and tears of the child.

מָארֵיהּ דְּעָלְמָא, כְּתִיב בְּאוֹרַיְיתָא, כִּי יִקָּרֵא קַן צִפּוֹר לְפָנֶיךָ וְגוֹ׳ שַׁלֵּחַ תְּשַׁלַּח אֶת הָאֵם וְגוֹ׳. הֲוָה גָּעֵי הַהוּא יְנוּקָא וּבְכֵי, אָמַר, מָארֵיהּ דְּעָלְמָא, קַיֵּים מִלָּה דָּא דְּאוֹרַיְיתָא, תְּרֵין בְּנִין הֲוֵינָא מֵאַבָּא וְאִמִּי, אֲנָא וַאֲחוֹתִי זְעֵירְתָּא מִנַּאי. הֲוָה לָךְ לְמֵיסַב לָן, וּלְקַיְּימָא מִלָּה דְּאוֹרַיְיתָא. וְאִי תֵּימָא מָארֵיהּ דְּעָלְמָא, אִם כְּתִיב, וְלָא אָב, הָא הָכָא כּוֹלָּא הוּא, אַבָּא וְאִמָּא. אִימָּא מִיתַת, וּנְסִיבַת לָהּ מֵעַל בְּנִין. הַשְׁתָּא אַבָּא דַּהֲוֵי חָפֵי עֲלָן, אַנְסִיב מֵעַל בְּנִין, אָן דִּינָא דְּאוֹרַיְיתָא. בְּכוּ ר׳ אֶלְעָזָר וְחַבְרַיָּיא, לָקֳבֵל בִּכְיָה וְגָעוּ דְּהַהוּא יְנוּקָא.

Rav Elazar opened the discussion with the verse: "The heaven for height, and the earth for depth." As Rav Elazar spoke this verse, a pillar

362. פָּתַח ר׳ אֶלְעָזָר וְאָמַר, שָׁמַיִם לָרוּם וְאָרֶץ לָעוֹמֶק וְגוֹ׳. עַד דַּהֲוָה אָמַר ר׳ אֶלְעָזָר קְרָא דָּא, הֲוָה עַמּוּדָא דְּאֶשָּׁא פָּסִיק

of fire separated them from the departed, but the child was still attached to the lips of his father and did not separate. Rav Elazar said, "Either God wishes to perform a miracle and revive the father of this child, or He desires that no one else approach the body. However, I cannot bear to see the child's tears or hear his words."

While still sitting, they heard another voice that said: "Blessed are you, Rav Yosi, that the words of the young kid and his tears rose to the throne of God and removed the decree. And God delivered thirteen people in your stead to the Angel of Death. Behold, they have added 22 years to your life, so you will have time to teach the young kid, the perfect and beloved, before the Creator."

Rav Elazar and the friends rose and did not allow anyone to stay in the house. They saw that the pillar of fire was gone. Rav Yosi opened his eyes and the child was still pressed with his lips to his lips.

בֵּינַיְיהוּ, וְהַהוּא יַנּוּקָא הֲוָה דָּבִיק בְּפוּמֵיהּ דַּאֲבוֹי, וְלָא הֲווֹ מִתְפָּרְשָׁאן. א'ר אֶלְעָזָר, אוֹ בָּעֵי קוּדְשָׁא בְּרִיךְ הוּא לְמִרְוַשׁ נִיסָא, אוֹ בָּעֵי דְּלָא יִשְׁתְּדַל בַּר נָשׁ אַחֲרָא עֲלֵיהּ, אֲבָל עַל מִלִּין דְּהַהוּא יַנּוּקָא וְדִמְעוֹי, לָא יָכִילְנָא לְמִסְבַּל.

363. עַד דַּהֲווֹ יַתְבִין, שָׁמְעוּ חַד קָלָא, דַּהֲוָה אָמַר, זַכָּאָה אַנְתְּ רִבִּי יוֹסֵי, דְּמִלִּין דְּהַאי גַּדְיָא וְדִמְעוֹי, וְדִמְעוֹי, סְלִיקוּ לְגַבֵּי כֻּרְסְיָיא דְּמַלְכָּא קַדִּישָׁא, וְדָנוּ דִּינָא, וְתְלֵיסַר בְּנֵי נָשָׁא אַזְמִין קוּדְשָׁא בְּרִיךְ הוּא לְמַלְאָךְ הַמָּוֶת בְּגִינָךְ, וְהָא עֶשְׂרִין וּתְרֵין שְׁנִין אוֹסִיפוּ לָךְ, עַד דְּתוֹלִיף אוֹרַיְיתָא, לְהַאי גַּדְיָא שְׁלֵימָא, וַחֲבִיבָא קַמֵּי קוּדְשָׁא בְּרִיךְ הוּא.

364. קָמוּ ר' אֶלְעָזָר וְחַבְרַיָּיא, וְלָא שָׁבְקוּ לְבַר נָשׁ לְמֵיקָם בְּבֵיתָא, מִיָּד וְזָמוּ הַהוּא עַמּוּדָא דְּאֶשָׁא דְּסָלִיק, וְר' יוֹסֵי פָּתַח עֵינוֹי. וְהַהוּא יַנּוּקָא דָּבִיק פּוּמֵיהּ בְּפוּמֵיהּ.

Rav Elazar said, "Blessed is our lot that with our own eyes we witnessed the resurrection of the dead." They approached Rav Yosi and the child fell asleep, as if he were expiring from this world. They said, "Blessed is your lot, Rav Yosi, and blessed is the Merciful One, who due to the crying and weeping of your son has performed a miracle for your sake. He was pushing open the gates of heaven with his beautiful words, and life was added to you because of his pleading and his tears."

א"ר אֶלְעָזָר, זַכָּאָה וְחוּלָקָנָא דְּוָזוֹמֵינָא תְּוֹזַיַית הַמֵּתִים, עֵינָא בְּעֵינָא. קְרִיבוּ לְגַבֵּיהּ, וַהֲוָה הַהוּא יַנּוּקָא נָאִים, כְּמָה דְּגָוַע מֵהַאי עָלְמָא, אָמְרוּ זַכָּאָה וְחוּלָקָךְ רַבִּי יוֹסֵי, וּבְרִיךְ רַחֲמָנָא דְּאַרְוִוַיַּיש לָךְ נִיסָא, עַל גַּעְיָא וּבְכְיָיא דִּבְנָךְ, וּבְמִלּוֹי, דְּהָכִי דָּוְוַיק בְּמִלִּין שַׁפִּירִין לְתְרַע שְׁמַיָּא, בְּמִלּוֹי וּבְדְמָעוֹי אוֹסִיפוּ לָךְ וַיְּיָן.

They took the child and kissed him and cried with him in great joy. They removed him to another house and woke him up from his sleep. They did not inform him immediately of his father's return to life, but did so later on. They rejoiced there for three days and revealed, with Rav Yosi, many new secrets in the Torah.

365. נְטָלוּהוּ לְהַהוּא יַנּוּקָא, וּנְשַׁקוּהוּ וּבְכוּ עֲמֵיהּ מֵוֶזֶדְוָה סַגְּיָא. וְאַפְקוּהוּ לְבֵיתָא אַוֹזֲרָא, וְאִתְּעָרוּ עֲלֵיהּ, וְלָא אוֹדְעוּ לֵיהּ מִיָּד, אֶלָּא לְבָתַר הָכִי. וַוְדוֹ תַּמָּן תְּלָתָא יוֹמִין, וְוָזַדִּישׁוּ בַּהֲדֵי הַהוּא רַבִּי יוֹסֵי, כַּמָה וֹזַדּוּשִׁין בְּאוֹרַיְיתָא.

Rav Yosi said to them, "Friends, I was not given authority to reveal what I observed in that world, until twelve years have passed.

366. אָמַר לוֹן ר' יוֹסֵי, וַזֲבְרַיָּיא, לָא אִתְיְהִיבַת לִי רְשׁוּ לְגַלָּאָה מֵהַהוּא דְּוָזֲמֵינָא בְּהַהוּא עָלְמָא, אֶלָּא לְבָתַר תְּרֵיסַר שְׁנִין.

"However, the 365 tears that my son wept were accounted before God. And I tell you, friends, at the time my son spoke that verse of the Torah, and cried out with those words, 300,000 benches that were in the heavenly academy were shaken. All the souls stood before God and asked for compassion towards me, and were guarantors for me that I would not sin during the time granted to me. The Creator was filled with compassion for me.

"The words of my son, and the way in which he gave up his soul for me, were pleasing to God. An angel was present there, who said, 'Master of the world, does it not say: 'Out of the mouth of babes and sucklings have You established strength against Your enemies, that You might still the enemy and the avenger?' May it please You that through the merit of the Torah, and the merit of that child who was ready to give his soul for his father's sake, You should have mercy on him and he should be saved.

אֲבָל תְּלַת מְאָה וְשִׁתִּין וַחֲמֵשׁ דִּמְעִין, דְּאוֹשִׁיד בְּרִי, עָאלוּ בְּווֹשְׁבָּנָא קַמֵּי מַלְכָּא קַדִּישָׁא, וְאוֹמֵינָא לְכוּ חַבְרַיָּיא, דִּבְשַׁעֲתָא דְּפָתַח בְּהַהוּא פְּסוּקָא, וְגָעָא בְּאִינּוּן מִלִּין, אִזְדַּעֲזְעוּ תְּלַת מְאָה אַלְפֵי סַפְסְלֵי דַּהֲווֹ בִּמְתִיבְתָּא דִּרְקִיעָא, וְכֻלְּהוּ קַיְימֵי קַמֵּיהּ דְּמַלְכָּא קַדִּישָׁא, וּבָעוּ רַחֲמֵי עֲלַי, וְעָרְבוּ לִי. וְקוּדְשָׁא בְּרִיךְ הוּא אִתְמְלֵי רַחֲמִין עֲלַי.

367. וְשַׁפִּיר קַמֵּיהּ, אִינּוּן מִלִּין, וְהֵיךְ מָסַר נַפְשֵׁיהּ עֲלַי. וְזֵד אַפְּטְרוּפְסָא הֲוָה קַמֵּיהּ, וְקָאֲמַר, מָארֵי דְּעָלְמָא, הָא כְּתִיב מִפִּי עוֹלְלִים וְיוֹנְקִים יִסַּדְתָּ עֹז לְמַעַן צוֹרְרֶיךָ לְהַשְׁבִּית אוֹיֵב וּמִתְנַקֵּם. יְהֵא רַעֲוָא קַמָּךְ, וְזָכוּ דְּאוֹרַיְיתָא, וְזָכוּ דְּהַהוּא רַבְיָא, דְּקָא מָסַר נַפְשֵׁיהּ עַל אֲבוּהּ דְּתֵיחוּס עֲלֵיהּ, וְיִשְׁתֵּזִיב.

"Thirteen people were pre-pared and delivered to the Angel of Death in my stead. Then God called on the Angel of Death and instructed him to return after 22 years, because those thirteen who ransomed me did not excuse me from death forever. They were merely placed in the hands of the Angel of Death as temporary custodians. Now, friends, because God saw that you were truly just, the miracle occurred before your eyes."

368. וּתְלֵיסָר בְּנֵי נָשָׁא אַזְמִין לֵיהּ תְּווֹתִי, וְעֶרְבוֹנָא יָהַב לֵיהּ, מִדִּינָא תַּקִּיפָא דָּא. כְּדֵין קָרָא קוּדְשָׁא בְּרִיךְ הוּא לְמַלְאַךְ הַמָּוֶת, וּפָקִיד לֵיהּ עֲלֵי, דְּלֵיתִב לְבָתַר עֶשְׂרִין וּתְרֵין שְׁנִין, דְּהָא לָאו עֶרְבּוֹנָא קַמֵּיהּ, אֶלָּא לֵיתוּב לִידוֹי, מַשְׁכְּנִין דַּהֲווֹ בִּידוֹי, הַשְׁתָּא וּלְבָרַיָּיא, בְּגִין דְּחָזְמָא קוּדְשָׁא בְּרִיךְ הוּא דְּאַתּוּן זַכָּאֵי קְשׁוֹט, אִתְרְחִישׁ נִיסָא לְעֵינַיְיכוּ.

MEDITATION

By meditating on this section we kindle appreciation for the power that resides within each one of us, and we awaken that power to do even greater things than we could ever imagine.

זַכָּאָה אַנְתְּ רַבִּי יוֹסֵי, דְּמִלִּין דְּהַאי גַּדְיָא זְעֵירָא,
ze'eira gadya dehai demilin Yosei Ribbi ant zaka'ah

וְדִמְעוֹי, סְלִיקוּ לְגַבֵּי כֻּרְסְיָיא דְּמַלְכָּא קַדִּישָׁא,
kadisha demalka kurseya legabei selika vedimoi

וְדָנוּ דִּינָא
dina vedanu

Blessed are you, Rav Yosi, that the words of the young kid and his tears rose to the throne of God and removed the decree.

OVERCOMING FEAR:

"A FORMIDABLE MOUNTAIN"

(ZOHAR, VAYECHI, VERSE 423)

If we're honest about it, probably many things frighten us. From our birth until the day we leave this world, fear is a constant challenge in our lives. As the Zohar explains, we experience the feeling of fear because of our lack of spiritual connection. These passages from the Zohar discuss traveling, but they are really about the whole of life's journey. As we make that journey, we should draw a connection to the Light every step of the way.

While traveling, Rav Yosi, Rav Yehuda, and Rav Chizkiyah encounter a formidable mountain. Rav Yosi is initially afraid of the danger they may encounter. But Rav Yehuda explains that as long as we are connected to the *Shechinah* there is no reason to fear. The term *Shechinah*, which is often used in the Zohar, refers to the female aspect of the Light of the Creator. The *Shechinah* is our spiritual mother, our surrounding, manifestable light, our protector, our sustainer. She is the source of all the Light and blessings that we draw into our lives. Hence, Rav Yehuda stresses the importance of consciously connecting ourselves to the *Shechinah* to draw protection to ourselves.

Early in this section, Rav Yosi refers to the prophet Samuel's fear when God told him to find a replacement for King Saul. When God asked why Samuel was hesitant to begin that search, Samuel replied that King Saul would kill him if King

Saul learned of Samuel's mission. Rav Yehuda explains that the situation of the three friends is different in that they are not alone, there is no imminent or obvious danger, and they are connected to the Light through their spiritual work. In other words, the *Shechinah* is with them.

While they were walking, they reached a mountain. Rav Yosi said, "This mountain is formidable, let us not remain here but walk on." Rav Yehuda said, "If you were solitary, I would advise it, for we have learned that he who walks alone on the road endangers his life, but this does not apply to three. Also, each of us is worthy that the *Shechinah* will not depart from us."

Rav Yosi said, "We have learned that a man should not rely on a miracle. We know this from Samuel, as it is written: 'How can I go? If Saul hears it, he will kill me,' and Samuel was more worthy than us." Rav Yehuda said to him: "Though he was more worthy of a miracle than we are, he was alone, and the danger was obvious. But we are three, and there is no danger in sight. If there will be evil spirits, we have learned that they do not appear before or cause harm to a group of three; nor are there robbers here, since the mountain is far from inhabited places, and there are no people here, but it is true there are wild beasts here."

423. עַד דַּהֲווֹ אָזְלֵי, אַעֲלוּ בְּחַד טוּרָא, א'ר יוֹסֵי, הַאי טוּרָא דַחֲזֵינָא, גֵּדַּךְ וְלָא נִתְעַכֵּב הָכָא, בְּגִין דְטוּרָא דַּחֲזִילָא הוּא. אָמַר רִבִּי יְהוּדָה, אִי הֲוָה וַד, הֲוָה אֲמֵינָא הָכֵי, דְּהָא תָּנֵינָן דְּמַאן דְּאָזֵיל יְחִידָאי בְּאוֹרְחָא אִתְחַיַּיב בְּנַפְשֵׁיהּ, אֲבָל תְּלָתָא לָא, וְכָל וַד וְוַד מִינָן, אִתְחֲזֵי דְּלָא תַּעֲדֵי מִינָן שְׁכִינְתָּא.

424. א'ר יוֹסֵי, הָא תָּנֵינָן דְּלָא יִסְמוֹךְ בַּר נָשׁ עַל נִסָּא. מִנָּלָן. מִשְּׁמוּאֵל, דִּכְתִיב אֵיךְ אֵלֵךְ וְשָׁמַע שָׁאוּל וַהֲרָגָנִי, וְהָא אִתְחֲזֵי שְׁמוּאֵל יַתִּיר מִינָן. אָמַר לֵיהּ, אֲפִילוּ הָכֵי, אִיהוּ הֲוָה וַד, וְהֶזֵּיקָא אִשְׁתְּכַח לְעֵינָא. אֲבָל אֲנַן תְּלָתָא, וְהֶזֵּיקָא לָא אִשְׁתְּכַח לְעֵינָא. דְּאִי מִשּׁוּם מַזִּיקִין. הָא תָּנֵינָן, דִּלְתִלְתָּא לָא מִתְחֲזֵי, וְלָא מַזְקֵי, וְאִי מִשּׁוּם לִסְטִים, לָא מִשְׁתַּכְּחֵי הָכָא, דְּהָא רָחֵיק מִיִּשׁוּבָא הַאי טוּרָא, וּבְנֵי נָשָׁא לָא מִשְׁתַּכְּחֵי הָכָא, בְּרַם דַּחֲוִילוּ הוּא, דְּחֵיוָון בָּרָא דְּמִשְׁתַּכְּחִין הָכָא.

Rav Yehuda continued the discussion saying: "'The angel who redeems...' It says 'redeems,' while it should have been 'who redeemed.' Why the present tense? This is because the angel abides always with people and never abandons a righteous man. Come and see: The angel who redeems me is the *Shechinah*, who continually accompanies man, never turning from him as long as he persists in the spiritual work. A man should therefore be careful not to go out alone on the road. What is 'alone?' A man should be careful to persist in the spiritual work, so that the *Shechinah* shall not depart from him, and he will have to go alone, unaccompanied by the *Shechinah*.

"Come and see: When a man sets out on his way, he should pray before God in order to draw the *Shechinah* upon him, and then go out on his way, joined by the *Shechinah*, who would redeem him on the way and save him in time of need.

425. פָּתַח וַאֲמַר הַמַּלְאָךְ הַגּוֹאֵל אוֹתִי מִכָּל רָע, הַאי קְרָא אִית לְאִסְתַּכְּלָא בֵּיהּ, הַגּוֹאֵל, אֲשֶׁר גָּאַל מִבָּעֵי לֵיהּ, מַאי הַגּוֹאֵל. בְּגִין דְּהוּא מִשְׁתַּכַּח תָּדִיר לְגַבֵּי בְּנֵי נָשָׁא, וְלָא אַעֲדֵי מב"נ זַכָּאָה לְעָלְמִין. תָּא חֲזֵי, הַמַּלְאָךְ הַגּוֹאֵל אוֹתִי דָּא שְׁכִינְתָּא, דְּאָזִיל עִמֵּיהּ דְּב"נ תָּדִיר, וְלָא אַעֲדֵי מִנֵּיהּ, כַּד ב"נ נָטִיר פִּקּוּדֵי אוֹרַיְיתָא. וְע"ד יִזְדַּהַר בַּר נָשׁ, דְּלָא יִפּוּק יְחִידָאי בְּאוֹרְחָא, מַאי יְחִידָאי. דְּיִזְדַּהַר ב"נ לְמִנְטַר פִּקּוּדֵי דְאוֹרַיְיתָא, בְּגִין דְּלָא תַעֲדֵי מִנֵּיהּ שְׁכִינְתָּא, וְיִצְטָרֵךְ לְמֵיזַל יְחִידָאי, בְּלָא זִוּוּגָא דִשְׁכִינְתָּא.

426. תָּא חֲזֵי, כַּד נָפִיק בַּר נָשׁ לְאוֹרְחָא, יְסַדֵּר צְלוֹתָא קַמֵּי מָארֵיהּ, בְּגִין לְאַמְשָׁכָא עֲלֵיהּ שְׁכִינְתָּא, וּלְבָתַר יִפּוּק לְאוֹרְחָא, וְיִשְׁתְּכַח זִוּוּגָא דִשְׁכִינְתָּא, לְמִפְרַק לֵיהּ בְּאוֹרְחָא, וּלְשֵׁזָבָא לֵיהּ, בְּכָל מַה דְּאִצְטָרִיךְ.

"It is written that Yaakov said: 'If God will be with me,' referring to the union with the *Shechinah* 'and will keep me in this way' to deliver him from any harm. Yaakov was solitary at the time, and the *Shechinah* walked before him. So much more for friends — that is, the righteous — with the words of the Torah among them."

427. מַה כְּתִיב בְּיַעֲקֹב, אִם יִהְיֶה אֱלֹקִים עִמָּדִי, דָּא זִוּוּגָא דִשְׁכִינְתָּא. וּשְׁמָרַנִי בַּדֶּרֶךְ הַזֶּה, לְמִפְרַק לִי מִכֹּלָּא, וְיַעֲקֹב יְחִידָאי הֲוָה בְּהַהוּא זִמְנָא, וּשְׁכִינְתָּא אָזְלַת קַמֵּיהּ, כָּל שֶׁכֵּן חַבְרַיָּא דְּאִית בֵּינַיְיהוּ מִלִּין דְּאוֹרַיְיתָא, עַל אַחַת כַּמָּה וְכַמָּה.

Rav Yosi said, "What shall we do? If we stay here, the day declines and if we climb, it is a great and formidable mountain and I fear the wild beasts." Rav Yehuda said, "I am amazed that you are so afraid." Rav Yosi said to him: "We have learned that a man should not rely on a miracle, since God does not perform miracles at all times." Rav Yehuda said to him: "This is true for a lone man, but we are three. With words of the Torah between us, and the *Shechinah* with us, I have no fear."

428. א'ר יוֹסֵי, מַאי נַעֲבֵיד, אִי נִתְעַכֵּב הָכָא, הָא יוֹמָא מָאִיךְ לְמֵיעַל, אִי נְהַךְ לְעֵילָא, טוּרָא רַב אִיהוּ, וּדְחִילוּ דְּחֵיוָון וַקְלָא דַּחֲוֵילְנָא. א'ר יְהוּדָה, תְּוּוהְנָא עֲלָךְ ר יוֹסֵי. א'ל הָא תָּנִינָן דְּלָא יִסְמוֹךְ בַּר נָשׁ עַל נִסָּא, דְּקוּדְשָׁא בְּרִיךְ הוּא לָא יַרְוֵיֵישׁ נִסָּא בְּכָל שַׁעְתָּא. א'ל ה'ם יְחִידָאי, אֲבָל אֲנַחְנָא תְּלָתָא, וּמִלֵּי אוֹרַיְיתָא בֵּינָנָא, וּשְׁכִינְתָּא עִמָּנָא, לָא דַחֲוֵילְנָא.

MEDITATION

As you read these words from the Zohar, think about things in your life that cause you to be afraid. The connection with the *Shechinah* that this meditation imparts will help you in the process of overcoming your fears. This meditation also brings the understanding that, to be permanently free of fear, we need to continuously strengthen our connection to the Creator's Light. Fear literally cannot exist when our connection with the *Shechinah* is strong.

וּמִלֵּי אוֹרַיְיתָא בֵּינָנָא, וּשְׁכִינְתָא עִמָּנָא,
imana ushchinta beinana orayita umilei

לָא דָחֵילְנָא
dacheilna la

With words of the Torah between us, and the Shechinah with us, I have no fear.

When You Need Protection:

"And the fear of you and the dread of you"

(Zohar, Noach, verse 252)

We spoke about fears in the previous section. Here the Zohar teaches us how complete protection can be achieved.

Not every fear is irrational. There are things you really ought to be afraid of—but that doesn't mean you should let yourself be dominated by those things. On the contrary, the Zohar teaches that each of us is born with a protective shield of Light, the Tzelem Elokim, that surrounds each body like an aura. When this shield is strong, healthy, and functioning at maximum power, even the genuinely dangerous and frightening powers in the world (symbolized in this section by wild animals) retreat from us.

It's also true, however, that negative actions can weaken and dim the protective shield of Light. This arouses fear within us—and the fear is not at all irrational, because our negative actions really have made us more vulnerable to destructive external forces.

Once we understand this, the practical importance of spiritual work becomes clear. Overcoming our negative impulses and doing our spiritual work through acts of sharing are not just virtuous actions. In a very practical way, this strengthens our defenses against the real dangers that life presents.

"And the fear of you and the dread of you shall be" means that from now on, you shall take the form of human beings. Now come and behold: In the beginning it is written: 'For in the image of God, He made man,' and also, 'In the likeness of God, He made him.' The wild beasts were afraid of human beings, but when people performed negative actions, they no longer maintained the supernal image, and they became afraid of the beasts of the field.

Formerly, the creatures of the world looked upon Man and saw the holy supernal image and trembled with fear. But as people sinned, their image was transformed in the eyes of the beasts. This is why human beings now tremble with fear of other creatures.

Come and behold: All the people who do not behave negatively before their Master, and do not transgress against the spiritual laws, retain the Divine splendor of the image of the Creator.

252. וּמוֹרַאֲכֶם וְחִתְּכֶם יִהְיֶה. מִכָּאן וּלְהָלְאָה, יְהֵא לְכוֹן דְּיוֹקְנִין דִּבְנֵי נָשָׁא, דְּהָא בְּקַדְמֵיתָא לָא הֲווֹ דְּיוֹקְנִין דִּבְנֵי נָשָׁא. תָּא וַחֲזֵי, בְּקַדְמֵיתָא כְּתִיב בְּצֶלֶם אֱלֹקִים עָשָׂה אֶת הָאָדָם. וּכְתִיב בִּדְמוּת אֱלֹקִים עָשָׂה אוֹתוֹ. כֵּיוָן דְּיָזְטוֹ אִשְׁתַּנּוּ דְּיוֹקְנַיְיהוּ, מֵהַהוּא דְּיוֹקְנָא עִלָּאָה, וְאִתְהַפְּכוּ אִינּוּן לְמִדְחַל מִקַּמֵּי חֵיוָון בְּרָא.

253. בְּקַדְמֵיתָא, כָּל בִּרְיָן דְּעָלְמָא, זַקְפָן עַיְינִין, וְחָמָאן דְּיוֹקְנָא, קַדִּישָׁא עִלָּאָה, וְזָעָאן וְדַחֲלִין מִקַּמֵּיהּ. כֵּיוָן דְּיָזְטוֹ אִתְהַדָּר דְּיוֹקְנַיְיהוּ, בְּעֵינַיְיהוּ, לְדְיוֹקְנָא אָחֳרָא. וְאִתְהַפָּךְ דִּבְנֵי נָשָׁא זָעִין וְדַחֲלִין קַמֵּי שְׁאַר בִּרְיָן.

254. תָּא וַחֲזֵי, כָּל אִינּוּן בְּנֵי נָשָׁא, דְּלָא וָזָטָאן קַמֵּי מָארֵיהוֹן, וְלָא עָבְרִין עַל פִּקּוּדֵי אוֹרַיְיתָא.

Therefore all the creatures of the world tremble with fear before them. But when the people transgress against the spiritual laws, their shape changes and they themselves tremble with fear of other creatures, because the supernal shape has left them. Because the beasts cannot see the supernal form in them anymore, they are ruled by the beasts of the field.

זִיו דְּיוֹקְנָא דִּלְהוֹן, לָא אִשְׁתְּנֵי מֵחֵיזוּ דְּדִיוֹקְנָא עִלָּאָה. וְכָל בִּרְיָין דְּעָלְמָא, זָעִין וְדָחֲלִין קַמֵּיהּ. וּבְשַׁעֲתָא דִּבְנֵי נָשָׁא עָבְרִין עַל פִּתְגָּמֵי אוֹרַיְיתָא, אִתְחַלַּף דְּיוֹקְנָא דִּלְהוֹן, וְכֻלְּהוּ זָעִין וְדָחֲלִין מִקַּמֵּי בִּרְיָין אוֹחֲרָנִין, בְּגִין דְּאִתְחַלַּף דְּיוֹקְנָא עִלָּאָה, וְאִתְעֲבַר מִנַּיְיהוּ, וּכְדֵין שָׁלְטֵי בְּהוֹ חֵיוַת בְּרָא, דְּהָא לָא חֲזוֹ בְּהוֹ, הַהוּא דְּיוֹקְנָא עִלָּאָה כִּדְקָחֲזֵי.

When the people left the ark and the world was renewed, God blessed them by granting them dominion over all creatures, even over the fish in the sea. As it is written: "And upon all the fish of the sea; into your hand they are delivered." Rav Chiya said, "'Into your hand they are delivered' indicates that when God created the world, He delivered everything into the hands of man. As it is written: 'And have dominion over the fish of the sea, and over the fowl of the air...'"

255. וְעַל כָּךְ, הַשְׁתָּא כֵּיוָן דְּעָלְמָא אִתְחַדַּשׁ כְּמִלְּקַדְמִין, בָּרִיךְ לוֹן, בִּרְכְתָא דָא, וְשַׁלְּיט לוֹן עַל כֹּלָּא, כד"א וְכָל דְּגֵי הַיָּם בְּיֶדְכֶם נִתָּנוּ. וַאֲפִילוּ נוּנֵי יַמָּא. ר' חִיָּיא אָמַר, בְּיֶדְכֶם נִתָּנוּ. מִקַּדְמַת דְּנָא. דְּכַד בָּרָא קֻדְשָׁא בְּרִיךְ הוּא עָלְמָא מְסַר כֹּלָּא בִּידֵהוֹן, דִּכְתִיב, וּרְדוּ בִּדְגַת הַיָּם וּבְעוֹף הַשָּׁמַיִם וְגוֹ'.

MEDITATION

Ultimately, we can reach a state of being in which nothing can harm us. This meditation strengthens our protective shield and inspires us to avoid actions that weaken it.

תָּא חֲזֵי, כָּל אִינוּן בְּנֵי נָשָׁא, דְּלָא חָטָאן
chataan dela nasha benei inun kol chazei ta

קַמֵּי מָארֵיהוֹן, וְלָא עָבְרִין עַל פִּקּוּדֵי אוֹרַיְיתָא.
orayita pikudei al avrin vela mareihon kamei

זִיו דְּיוֹקְנָא דִּלְהוֹן, לָא אִשְׁתַּנֵּי מֵחֵיזוּ דְּדִיוֹקְנָא
didyokna mecheizu ishtanei la dilhon deyokna ziv

עִלָּאָה. וְכָל בְּרִיָּין דְּעָלְמָא, זָעִין וְדָחֲלִין
vedachalin zayin de'alma beriyan vechol ila'ah

קַמֵּיהּ.
kameih

Come and behold: All the people who do not behave negatively before their Master, and do not transgress against the spiritual laws, retain the Divine splendor of the image of the Creator. Therefore all the creatures of the world tremble with fear before them.

THE POWER OF FORGIVENESS
TO REMOVE JUDGMENT:
"RAV ABA AND THE TRAVELER"
(ZOHAR, MIKETZ, VERSE 186)

How many times in your life have you felt the desire to hurt someone, for the simple reason that they hurt you first? Whenever you try to enact vengeance, even if you truly feel it's justified, you create an opening for judgment to be enacted upon yourself. But when you resist an impulse for reactive vengeance, you bring forgiveness and good will into your life.

Sometimes the Zohar is challenging in its teachings, and sometimes it is straightforward. This section uses a simple, clear story to reveal the power of true forgiveness. The traveler in this section was not even aware of the two miracles that had saved him from danger. But it was the power of forgiveness he had practiced throughout his life that protected him. Rav Aba learns of this power from the traveler, and we in turn are taught by Rav Aba.

As Rav Aba sat by the gate of the city Lod, he saw a traveler standing near the edge of a cliff on the mountainside. The traveler must have been weary from the road, for as Rav Aba watched, he lay down and slept. While he was sleeping, a snake came toward him. Then a lizard suddenly appeared and killed the snake. When the traveler awoke, he saw the dead snake and stepped back from the cliff. Just then the cliff was torn from the mountainside and fell to the valley below, but the traveler was saved. If he had awakened a moment later, he would have fallen to his death.

186. ר' אַבָּא הֲוָה יָתִיב אַתַּרְעָא דְּאַבָּבָא דְלוֹד, וְחָמָא חַד בַּר נָשׁ דַּהֲוָה אָתֵי, וְיָתִיב בְּווֹד קוּלְטָא דְתִכְלָא דְאַרְעָא, וַהֲוָה לָאֵי מֵאָרְחָא, וְיָתִיב וְנָאֵים תַּמָּן, אַדְּהֲכֵי וְחָמֵי חַד חִוְיָא, דַּהֲוָה אָתֵי לְגַבֵּיהּ, נָפַק קוּסְטָפָא דְגוּרְדְּנָא, וְקָטִיל לֵיהּ לְחִוְיָא. כַּד אִתְעַר הַהוּא בַּר נָשׁ, וְחָמָא הַהוּא חִוְיָא לְקָבְלֵיהּ, דַּהֲוָה מִית, אוֹדְקַף הַהוּא בַּר נָשׁ, וְנָפַל הַהוּא קוּלְטָא לְעוּמְקָא דִּתְחוֹתוֹי וְאִשְׁתֵּזִיב.

Rav Aba approached the traveler and said: "What have you done that the Holy One, blessed be He, performed two miracles for you: saving you from the snake, and saving you from the falling cliff? For these events did not happen without a reason."

187. אָתָא ר' אַבָּא לְגַבֵּיהּ, אָמַר לוֹ אֵימָא לִי מָאן עוֹבָדָךְ, דְּהָא קוּדְשָׁא בְּרִיךְ הוּא רָחִישׁ לָךְ אִלֵּין תְּרֵין נִסִּין, לָאו אִינוּן לְמַגָּנָא.

The traveler replied, "In all my days, I forgave and made peace with any man who did evil by me. If I could not make peace with him, I did not sleep on my bed before forgiving him and all others who had aggrieved me, and I did not harbor hatred for any harm that had been done to me. Moreover, from that day on, I tried to do kindness by them."

188. אָמַר לוֹ הַהוּא בַּר נָשׁ, בְּכָל יוֹמָאי לָא אַשְׁלִים לִי בַּר נָשׁ בִּישָׁא בְּעַלְמָא, דְּלָא אִתְפַּייְסְנָא בַּהֲדֵיהּ, וּמוֹזִילְנָא לֵיהּ. וְתוּ, אִי לָא יְכִילְנָא לְאִתְפַּייְסָא בַּהֲדֵיהּ, לָא סָלִיקְנָא לְעַרְסִי, עַד דִּמְוֹזִילְנָא לֵיהּ, וּלְכָל אִינוּן דִּמְצַעֲרוּ לִי, וְלָא וַיְישָׁעֲנָא כָּל יוֹמָא לְהַהוּא בִּישָׁא דְּאַשְׁלִים לִי. וְלָאו דִּי לִי דָא, אֶלָּא דְּמֵהַהוּא יוֹמָא וּלְהָלְאָה, אִשְׁתַּדַּלְנָא לְמֶעֱבַּד עִמְּהוֹן טָבָא.

Rav Aba wept and said: "This man's deeds exceed those of Yosef, for those who injured Yosef were his brothers. Assuredly, he should have pitied and forgiven them from brotherhood. But this man was forgiving of everyone, so he is greater than Yosef and is worthy to have the Holy One, blessed be He, perform one miracle after the other for his sake."

189. בָּכָה ר' אַבָּא וַאֲמַר, יַתִּיר עוֹבְדוֹי דְּדֵין מִיּוֹסֵף, דְּיוֹסֵף הֲווֹ אֲחוֹי וַדַּאי, וַהֲוָה לֵיהּ לְרַחֲמָא עֲלוֹי, אֲבָל מַה דַּעֲבִיד דָּא, יַתִּיר הוּא מִיּוֹסֵף, יָאוֹת הוּא דְּקוּדְשָׁא בְּרִיךְ הוּא יַרְוַוֵיט לֵיהּ נִיסָא עַל נִיסָא.

MEDITATION

Everything that happens to you is the effect of something you have done in this lifetime, or even in a former one—or it may be an experience that is being given to you to assist in your transformation. In either case, what takes place is *exactly* what you need at that moment.

Once you understand this, forgiveness for those who have "wronged" you is easy. In fact, vengeance will even be replaced by gratitude. Meditate on this section to awaken your ability for truly forgiving others.

כָּל יוֹמַאי לָא אַשְׁלֵים לִי בַּר נָשׁ בִּישָׁא
bisha bash bar li ashleim la yomai kol

בְּעָלְמָא, דְּלָא אִתְפַּייְסְנָא בַּהֲדֵיהּ, וּמְוזִילְנָא לֵיהּ.
leih umachilna bahadeih itpayasna dela be'alma

וְתוּ, אִי לָא יְכִילְנָא לְאִתְפַּייְסָא בַּהֲדֵיהּ, לָא סָלֵיקְנָא
salekna la bahadeih leitpaysa yachilna la i vetu

לְעַרְסִי, עַד דִּמְוזִילְנָא לֵיהּ, וּלְכָל אִינוּן דִּמְצַעֲרוּ
dimtza'aru inun ulechol leih demachilna ad le'arsi

לִי, וְלָא וַזְיִישְׁנָא כָּל יוֹמָא לְהָהוּא בִּישָׁא
bisha lehahu yuma kol chayshana vela li

דְּאַשְׁלֵים לִי. וְלָאו דִּי לִי דָא, אֶלָּא דִּמְהַהוּא יוֹמָא
yoma dimhahu ela da li di velau li de'ashleim

וּלְהָלְאָה, אִשְׁתַּדַּלְנָא לְמֶעְבַּד עִמְּהוֹן טָבָא.
tava imhon leme'evad ishtadalna ulehalah

In all my days, I forgave and made peace with any man who did evil by me. If I could not make peace with him, I did not sleep on my bed before forgiving him and all others who had aggrieved me, and I did not harbor hatred for any harm that had been done to me. Moreover, from that day on, I tried to do kindness by them.

FINDING LIGHT IN THE DARKNESS:

"RAV SHIMON'S DEPARTURE FROM THE CAVE"

(ZOHAR, PROLOGUE, VERSE 185)

When we find ourselves in difficult or dark situations, we may wonder why life has taken these turns. Yet even in darkness, Light can be revealed. A simple example makes this point powerfully: Nothing is more painful than the experience of giving birth, but through this pain life is brought into the world. This principle—that darkness is only a covering of the Light within—is one of the Zohar's most inspiring teachings.

The Zohar tells the story of how Rav Shimon was forced into hiding by the Romans; who had prohibited the teaching of this wisdom. In fact, Rav Shimon's master, Rav Akiva, had been killed for doing so. Rav Shimon and his son Rav Elazar ran away to the mountains, where they hid in a cave for thirteen years and studied.

In the passage below, Rav Pinchas, Rav Shimon's father-in-law, visits his friend Rav Rechumai. Using the symbol of a jewel, Rav Rechumai praises the spiritual radiance of Rav Shimon and Rav Elazar. As Rav Pinchas departs, he encounters two birds who deliver a message that Rav Shimon has emerged from the cave.

Rav Pinchas hurries to meet Rav Shimon and his son. They had been hiding there for thirteen years. Throughout the years of hiding, the Zohar tells us, Rav Shimon was buried neck deep in the ground. It was during this time that the Zohar was revealed to Rav Shimon. Though battered and decomposed, he is joyful and fulfilled. The difficulty Rav Shimon endured brought great Light to him and to the world.

Rav Pinchas often visited Rav Rechumai, who lived at the shore of Lake Kinneret. Rav Rechumai was a great man, but he was full of years and had lost his eyesight. He said to Rav Pinchas, "I have heard that our friend Yochai has a jewel, a precious stone. That is, he has a son. I have observed the light that shines from that jewel. It shines like the radiance of the sun as it emerges out of its sheath and illuminates the whole world.

"That light will reach down from the heavens to brighten the whole world, until the Ancient of Days appears and is properly seated upon the Throne. In your household, Rav Pinchas, that radiance is present in its entirety. And from this light in your household a tiny ray has come forth and it brightens the whole world. How happy is your lot! Go my son, go! Go to that jewel that lights up all the world, for the hour is right."

Then Rav Pinchas departed from Rav Rechumai.

185. רַבִּי פִּינְחָס הֲוָה שְׁכִיחַ
קַמֵּי דְּרַבִּי רְחוּמָאי בְּכֵיף יַמָּא
דְּגִנּוֹסַר. וּב"ג רַב וּקְשִׁישָׁא
דְּיוֹמִין הֲוָה, וְעֵינוֹי אִסְתַּלָּקוּ
מִלְּמֶחֱזֵי. אָמַר לְרַבִּי פִּינְחָס,
וַדַּאי שְׁמַעְנָא דְּיוֹחָאי חַבְרָנָא
אִית לֵיהּ מַרְגָּלִית אֶבֶן טָבָא,
וְאִסְתַּכְּלִית בִּנְהוֹרָא דְּהַהִיא
מַרְגָּלִית, נָפְקָא כִּנְהִירוּ
דְּשִׁמְשָׁא מִנַּרְתְּקָהּ, וְנָהֲרָא כָּל
עָלְמָא.

186. וְהַהוּא נְהוֹרָא קָאִים
מִשְּׁמַיָּא לְאַרְעָא, וְנָהִיר כָּל
עָלְמָא, עַד דְּיָתִיב עַתִּיק יוֹמִין,
וְיָתִיב עַל כָּרְסַיָּא כִּדְקָא
יָאוֹת. וְהַהוּא נְהוֹרָא כָּלִיל
כֹּלָּא בְּבֵיתָךְ, וּמִנְּהוֹרָא
דְּאִתְכְּלִיל בְּבֵיתָךְ, נָפִיק נְהִירוּ
דַּקִּיק וְזָעֵיר, וְנָפִיק לְבַר וְנָהִיר
כָּל עָלְמָא, זַכָּאָה וְזוּגְלָךְ. פּוּק
בְּרִי פּוּק, זִיל אֲבַתְרֵיהּ דְּהַהִיא
מַרְגָּלִית דְּנָהִיר עָלְמָא, דְּהָא
שַׁעֲתָא קָיְימָא לָךְ.

187. נָפַק מִקַּמֵּיהּ וְקָאִים
לְמֵיעַל בְּהַהִיא אַרְבָּא,

Accompanied by two people, Rav Pinchas was preparing to board a ship when he saw two birds flying toward him across the lake. Rav Pinchas raised his voice and said: "Birds, O birds—you who fly over the waters — have you seen the place where the son of Yochai is?" He waited awhile and then said: "Birds, O birds — go and bring me back an answer!" They flew away into the middle of the sea and disappeared.

Then, before Rav Pinchas boarded the ship, the two birds reappeared. In the mouth of one bird was a letter informing him that Rav Shimon, the son of Yochai, had left the cave together with his son, Rav Elazar. When Rav Pinchas went to meet Rav Shimon, he saw that Rav Shimon had completely changed. His body was full of scars and sores from having stayed so long in the cave. Rav Pinchas wept with Rav Shimon and said: "Woe that I have seen you so." Rav Shimon replied, "O, how happy is my lot, that you have

וּתְרֵין גּוּבְרִין בַּהֲדֵיהּ וָחֲמָא תְּרֵין צִפְּרִין דַּהֲווֹ אַתְיָין וְטָסִין עַל יַמָּא, רָמָא לוֹן קָלָא וַאֲמַר, צִפְּרִין צִפְּרִין דְּאַתּוּן טָאסִין עַל יַמָּא וַחֲמֵיתוּן דּוּךְ דְּבַר יוֹחַאי תַּמָּן, אִשְׁתָּהֵי פּוּרְתָּא אֲמַר צִפְּרִין זִילוּ וַאֲתִיבוּ לִי. פָּרְחוּ וַאֲזִילוּ, עָאלוּ בְּיַמָּא וְאָזְלֵי לְהוֹן.

188. עַד דְּנָפַק, הָא אִינּוּן צִפְּרִין אַתְיָין, וּבְפוּמָא דְּוֹדָא מִנַּיְיהוּ פִּתְקָא וָדָא, וּכְתִיב בְּגַוֵּוהּ, דְּהָא בַּר יוֹחַאי נָפַק מִן מְעַרְתָּא, וְרִבִּי אֶלְעָזָר בְּרֵיהּ אֲזַל לְגַבֵּיהּ, וְאִשְׁתְּכַּחוּ לֵיהּ מְשַׁנְיָא, וְגוּפֵיהּ מַלְיָא וַחֲלוּדִין. בָּכָה בַּהֲדֵיהּ, וַאֲמַר, וַוי דַּחֲמֵיתִיךְ בְּכָךְ. אֲמַר, זַכָּאָה וְוֹלָקִי דַּחֲמֵית לִי בְּכָךְ, דְּאִלְמָלֵא לָא חֲמֵיתָא לִי בְּכָךְ לָא הֲוֵינָא בְּכָךְ. פָּתַח רִבִּי שִׁמְעוֹן בְּפִקּוּדֵי אוֹרַיְיתָא וַאֲמַר, פִּקּוּדֵי אוֹרַיְיתָא דִּיהַב

seen me so. Because had you not seen me so scarred, I would not be what I am!"

קָדוֹשׁ בָּרוּךְ הוּא לְיִשְׂרָאֵל כָּלְהוֹ בְּאוֹרַיְיתָא בְּאֹרַח כְּלַל כְּתִיבֵי.

MEDITATION

Use this meditation whenever you find yourself in a dark or difficult situation. It will help you to know that there is Light hidden in darkness—and even more important, it will help you to reveal that Light.

אֲמַר, זַכָּאָה וֹזּלָקִי דַּחֲמֵית לִי בְּכָךְ,

bechach li dachmeit chulaki zaka'ah amar

דְּאִלְמָלֵא לָא חֲמֵיתָא לִי בְּכָךְ לָא הֲוֵינָא בְּכָךְ.

bechach haveina la bechach li chameita la de'ilmale

O, how happy is my lot, that you have seen me so. Because had you not seen me so scarred, I would not be what I am!

WHEN YOU NEED TO REMOVE
ENVY AND JEALOUSY:

"DO NOT EAT THE BREAD OF ONE
WHO HAS AN EVIL EYE"

(ZOHAR, SHEMOT, VERSE 21)

What causes us to desire what others have? Often it's a feeling of emptiness or lack in ourselves. While the Evil Eye might be a new concept, we certainly have all felt jealousy and envy. Kabbalah teaches that those feelings create an energy and a force—the Evil Eye—that negatively influence us as well as those of whom we are jealous or envious.

People transfer this negative energy through their eyes—to physical objects, to food and drink, or to other people. In this section, the Zohar discusses the danger of eating the food of someone who has the Evil Eye. The Egyptians were able to control the Israelites because the Israelites partook of bread that had been infused with the Evil Eye. This concept is not limited to food or drink. Partaking of any enjoyment with a negative person is definitely something to avoid. We need to be aware of the Evil Eye's effects in every area of our lives—including the negativity that we ourselves may direct toward others.

Rav Chiya opened the discussion, saying: "Do not eat the bread of him who has an Evil Eye, because the bread or the benefits to be had from that person are worthless." When the people of Israel descended into Egypt, had they not tasted the bread of Egypt, they would not have been forsaken in exile and the Egyptians would not have been able to harm them.

21. וְאֵלֶּה שְׁמוֹת בְּנֵי יִשְׂרָאֵל. רְבִּי חִיָּיא פָּתַח, אַל תִּלְחַם אֶת לֶחֶם רַע עַיִן וְאַל תִּתְאָו לְמַטְעַמּוֹתָיו. אַל תִּלְחַם אֶת לֶחֶם רַע עַיִן, בְּגִין דְּנַהֲמָא אוֹ הֲנָאָה דְּהַהוּא בַּר נָשׁ דְּהֲוֵי רַע עַיִן, לָאו אִיהוּ כְּדַאי לְמֵיכַל וּלְאִתְהֲנֵי מִנֵּיהּ. דְּאִי כַּד נַחְתוּ יִשְׂרָאֵל לְמִצְרַיִם, לָא יִטְעֲמוּן נַהֲמָא דְּמִצְרָאֵי, לָא אִשְׁתְּבָקוּ בְּגָלוּתָא, וְלָא יְעִיקָן לוֹן מִצְרָאֵי.

Rav Yitzchak said to him: "But it was decreed that the people of Israel should be in exile, and this was to be fulfilled even if they had not eaten the bread of the Egyptians." Rav Chiya said to him: "All this is correct. But it was not decreed that the exile be in Egypt, since it is not written: 'Your seed will be a stranger in the land of Egypt' but rather, 'In a land that is not theirs.' And it could even be in a different land."

22. אָמַר לֵיהּ רְבִּי יִצְחָק, וְהָא גְּזֵרָא אִתְגְּזַר. א'ל, כֹּלָּא אִיהוּ כְּדְקָא יָאוּת, דְּהָא לָא אִתְגְּזַר בְּמִצְרַיִם דַּוְוקָא, דְּהָא לָא כְּתִיב כִּי גֵר יִהְיֶה זַרְעֲךָ בְּאֶרֶץ מִצְרַיִם, אֶלָּא בְּאֶרֶץ לֹא לָהֶם, וַאֲפִילוּ בְּאַרְעָא אָחֳרָא.

Rav Yitzchak said, "A person who has concern for his soul, for whom eating is infused

23. אָמַר ר' יִצְחָק, מַאן דְּאִיהוּ בַּעַל נֶפֶשׁ, דְּמֵיכְלֵיהּ יַתִּיר

with importance and con-
sciousness—or even a person
who eats simply to survive—
should be extremely vigilant.
If he meets a person who has
the evil eye, he should be
very careful not to eat that
person's bread. For there is
no worse bread in the world
than the bread of an Evil-
Eyed person."

מִשְׁאָר בְּנֵי נָשָׁא, אוֹ מַאן
דְּהוּא אָזִיל בָּתַר מֵעוֹי, אִי
אַעְרַע בְּהַהוּא רַע עַיִן, יְכוּס
גַּרְמֵיהּ וְלָא יֵיכוּל מִנַּהֲמָא
דִּילֵיהּ, דְּלֵית נַהֲמָא בִּישָׁא
בְּעָלְמָא, בַּר מֵהַהוּא לֶחֶם רַע
עַיִן, מַה כְּתִיב כִּי לֹא יוּכְלוּן
הַמִּצְרִים לֶאֱכֹל אֶת הָעִבְרִים
לֶחֶם כִּי תוֹעֵבָה הִיא לְמִצְרָיִם,
הָא לָךְ לֶחֶם רַע עַיִן.

MEDITATION

With this meditation we awaken awareness of the danger of jealousy, both from other people and from ourselves. We also protect ourselves from the Evil Eye from others.

אָמַר ר' יִצְחָק, מַאן דְּאִיהוּ בַּעַל נֶפֶשׁ,
nefesh ba'al de'ihu ma'an Yitzchak Ribbi amar

דְּמֵיכְלֵיהּ יַתִּיר מִשְׁאָר בְּנֵי נָשָׁא, אוֹ מַאן
ma'an o nasha benei mishar yatir demeichleih

דְּהוּא אָזִיל בָּתַר מֵעוֹי, אִי אַעֲרַע בְּהַהוּא רַע
ra behahu i'ara i meoi batar azil dehu

עַיִן, יְכוּס גַּרְמֵיהּ וְלָא יֵיכוּל מִנַּהֲמָא דִּילֵיהּ,
dileih minahama yechul vela garmeh ychus ayin

דְּלֵית נַהֲמָא בִּישָׁא בְּעָלְמָא, בַּר מֵהַהוּא לֶחֶם
lechem mehahu bar be'alma bisha nahama deleit

רַע עַיִן, מַה כְּתִיב כִּי לֹא יוּכְלוּן הַמִּצְרִים
haMitzrim yuchlun lo ki ketiv ma ayin ra

לֶאֱכֹל אֶת הָעִבְרִים לֶחֶם כִּי תוֹעֵבָה הִיא
hi to'evah ki lechem ha'ivrim et le'echol

לְמִצְרַיִם, הָא לָךְ לֶחֶם רַע עַיִן.
ayin ra lechem lach ha leMitzrayim

Rav Yitzchak said, "A person who has concern for his soul, for whom eating is infused with importance and consciousness—or even a person who eats simply to survive—should be extremely vigilant. If he meets a person who has the evil eye, he should be very careful not to eat that person's bread. For there is no worse bread in the world than the bread of an Evil-Eyed person.

Understanding the Opponent, the Source of All Chaos and Negativity:

"With all your heart, and with all your soul, and with all your might"

(Zohar, Trumah, verse 673)

Right now, is there an area of your life that seems to be out of control? It may be a financial problem, or a difficult relationship, or a concern for your health. We all experience problems in our lives, and Kabbalah teaches that none of these difficulties are merely incidental. Behind them is a force of energy brought into being by the Creator to give us the opportunity to overcome challenges. Without this Opponent to overcome, we would not be able to grow and achieve the purpose for which we came into this world.

Through the story of a king's son and a harlot, the Zohar explains that the Opponent is a negative force with a positive purpose. Resisting the harlot enables the prince to become king, and overcoming the Opponent enables us to achieve our true greatness.

As this section describes, whoever inclines us toward a negative reaction actually deserves our gratitude. They provide us with a chance, through our own efforts, to turn away from negativity, and by so doing to reveal Light. This is the true role of evil in the world. It provides an opportunity for us to become the cause and creator of our own Light, and thereby to fulfill our purpose in the world.

It is like a king who had an only son, and loved him exceedingly. And he commanded him with love not to come close to an evil woman, because anyone who approached her was not worthy to enter the king's palace. That son promised that he would lovingly do the will of his father.

Outside the king's palace was a harlot who was very beautiful to behold. After a few days, the king said: "I want to know my son's feelings toward me." He called that harlot and told her: "Go and entice my son, in order to test his feelings toward me." What did that harlot do? She went to the king's son and embraced him and kissed him and enticed him with all kinds of enticements. The son is as he should be and observes the commands of his father; he scolds her and does not listen to her and thrusts her away from him. Then the father rejoices with his son, brings him into the inner sanctum of his palace, and gives him

673. אֶלָּא, וַדַּאי רְעוּתֵיהּ דְּמָארֵיהּ עָבֵיד. לְמַלְכָּא דַּהֲוָה לֵיהּ בַּר יְחִידָאי, וַהֲוָה רָחִים לֵיהּ יַתִּיר, וּפָקִיד עֲלֵיהּ בִּרְחִימוּ, דְּלָא יִקְרַב גַּרְמֵיהּ לְאִתְּתָא בִּישָׁא, בְּגִין דְּכֹל מַאן דְּיִקְרַב לְגַבָּהּ, לָאו כְּדַאי אִיהוּ לְאַעֲלָא גּוֹ פָּלַטְרִין דְּמַלְכָּא. אוֹדֵי לֵיהּ הַהוּא בְּרָא, לְמֶעְבַּד רְעוּתֵיהּ דַּאֲבוֹי בִּרְחִימוּ.

674. בְּבֵיתָא דְּמַלְכָּא, לְבַר, הֲוַת חֲדָא זוֹנָה, יָאֶה בְּחֵיזוּ, וְשַׁפִּירָא בְּרֵיוָא. לְיוֹמִין אָמַר מַלְכָּא, בָּעֵינָא לְמִנְדַּע רְעוּתֵיהּ דִּבְרִי לְגַבָּאי. קָרָא לָהּ לְהַהִיא זוֹנָה, וְאָמַר לָהּ זִילִי וּתְפַתֵּי לִבְרִי, לְמִנְדַּע רְעוּתֵיהּ דִּבְרִי לְגַבָּאי. הַהִיא זוֹנָה מַאי עַבְדַת, אֲזַלַת אֲבַתְרֵיהּ דִּבְרֵיהּ דְּמַלְכָּא שָׁרָאת לְחַבְּקָא לֵיהּ וּלְנַשְּׁקָא לֵיהּ, וּלְפַתֵּי לֵיהּ בְּכַמָּה פִתּוּיִין. אִי הַהוּא בְּרָא יֵאוֹת, וְאָצֵית לְפִקּוּדָא דַּאֲבוֹי, גָּעַר בָּהּ, וְלָא אָצֵית לָהּ, וְדָחֵי לָהּ מִנֵּיהּ. כְּדֵין אֲבוֹי חַדֵּי בִּבְרֵיהּ, וְאָעִיל לֵיהּ לְגוֹ פַּרְגּוֹדָא דְּהֵיכָלֵיהּ, וְיָהִיב לֵיהּ מַתְּנָן וּנְבִזְבְּזָא וִיקָר סַגִּיאָ.

presents and gifts and great honor. Who caused all this honor for that son? We must say that it was the harlot.

מַאן גָּרִים כָּל הַאי יְקָר לְהַאי בְּרָא, הֲוֵי אֵימָא הַהִיא זוֹנָה.

Does that harlot deserve praise for this or not? Certainly she deserves praise in every respect, for she did the king's command and she awakened the king's love toward his son. Therefore, it is written: "And, behold, it was very good." 'And, behold, it was good' refers to the Angel of Life, while 'very' refers to the Angel of Death, who is also certainly very good, for he fulfills the command of his Master. Come and see: if there would not be this enticer, then the righteous would not inherit those supernal treasures that are their share in the World to Come.

675. וְהַהִיא זוֹנָה אִית לָה שְׁבָחָא בְּהַאי אוֹ לָאו. וַדַּאי שְׁבָחָא אִית לָה מִכָּל סִטְרִין. וַזד, דְּעַבְדַת פְּקוּדָא דְמַלְכָּא. וְזַד, דְּגַרְמַת לֵיהּ לְהַהוּא בְּרָא, לְכָל הַהוּא טִיבוּ, לְכָל הַאי רְוֹזִּמוּ דְּמַלְכָּא לְגַבֵּיהּ. וְעַ"ד כְּתִיב, וְהִנֵּה טוֹב מְאֹד. וְהִנֵּה טוֹב, דָּא מַלְאָךְ חַיִּים. מְאֹד, דָּא מַלְאָךְ הַמָּוֶת, דְּאִיהוּ וַדַּאי טוֹב מְאֹד, לְמַאן דְּאָצִית פְּקוּדִין דְּמָארֵיהּ. וְתָא וְחֲזֵי, אִי לָא יְהֵא הַאי מְקַטְרְגָא, לָא יַרְתוּן צַדִּיקַיָּא הָנֵי גְּנִזַּיָּא עִלָּאִין, דְּזְמִינִין לְיַרְתָא לְעָלְמָא דְאָתֵי.

Blessed are those who met this enticer and blessed are those who did not meet this enticer. Blessed are those who met him, and that were saved from him, for because of him they inherit all that is good and all those delights,

676. זַכָּאִין אִינוּן דְּאַעֲרָעוּ בְּהַאי מְקַטְרְגָא, וְזַכָּאִין אִינוּן דְּלָא אַעֲרָעוּ בֵּיהּ. זַכָּאִין אִינוּן דְּאַעֲרָעוּ בֵּיהּ, וְאִשְׁתְּזִיבוּ מִנֵּיהּ, דִּבְגִינֵיהּ יַרְתִין כָּל אִינוּן טָבִין, וְכָל אִינוּן עֲדוּנִין,

and all those pleasures of the World to Come.

וְכָל אִינוּן כִּסוּפִין דְּעָלְמָא
דְּאָתֵי, דְּעָלֵיהּ כְּתִיב עַיִן לֹא
רָאָתָה אֱלֹהִים זוּלָתְךָ.

MEDITATION

Realizing that you have the power to resist negativity
brings the responsibility of using that power. It might
seem easier to just accept the role of victim and see
yourself as helpless before your fate. Ultimately, however, the idea that we live in a chaotic, random universe
is the most negative and destructive viewpoint. While
it may seem hard in the moment to see the challenges
set out by the Opponent as gifts for us, this meditation
brings both that realization and the energy to act upon
it.

זַכָּאִין אִינּוּן דְּאַעְרָעוּ בְּהַאי מְקַטְרְגָא, וְזַכָּאִין אִינּוּן
inun vezakayin mekatrega behai de'ira'u inun zaka'in

דְּלָא אַעְרָעוּ בֵּיה. זַכָּאִין אִינּוּן דְּאַעְרָעוּ בֵּיה,
beih de'ira'u inun zakayin beh i'ara'n dela

וְאִשְׁתְּזִיבוּ מִנֵּיה, דִּבְגִינֵיה יָרְתִין כָּל אִינּוּן
inun kol yartin divgineih mineih ve'ishtezivu

טָבִין, וְכָל אִינּוּן עִדּוּנִין, וְכָל אִינּוּן כִּסּוּפִין
kisufin inun vechol idunin inun vechol tavin

דְּעָלְמָא דְּאָתֵי,
de'atei de'alma

*Blessed are those who met this enticer and blessed are those
who did not meet this enticer. Blessed are those who met
him, and that were saved from him, for because of him they
inherit all that good and all those delights, and all those
pleasures of the World to Come.*

Connecting to Your

Soul Mate

(Zohar, Lech Lecha, verse 346)

For many people, finding a soul mate is the most difficult task of their lives. Part of the difficulty comes from trying to find the right person rather than *being* the right person. Finding your soul mate isn't just a matter of going on many dates or networking to make new acquaintances. To draw the soul you desire, you need to become that level of soul yourself. This means developing yourself spiritually. It means doing the spiritual work the Zohar describes, and using the spiritual tools Kabbalah provides.

Here the Zohar reveals the mysteries surrounding male and female aspects of the soul, as well as the concept of soul mate relationships. When a complete soul enters this physical realm, it does so through the efforts of the angel *Lailah* (which in English means "Night"). During the process of descent from the Upper World, the unified soul separates into male and female halves. If the two halves of the soul embark on a spiritual path during physical existence, they can merit reunification. While the angel *Lailah* is responsible for bringing souls into the physical dimension, it is the Creator who reunites two halves of one soul when the time is right, for only the Creator knows with certainty who are true soul mates.

Come and behold: All the souls that are destined to come to the world appear before Him as couples, with each soul divided into male and female halves. Afterward, when the souls arrive in this world, the Holy One, blessed be He, matches them together. Rav Yitzchak said, "The Holy One says, 'The daughter of this man shall go with the son of that man.'"

Rav Yosi asked, "What is the meaning of this? How can the Holy One announce who goes with whom when the souls enter this world, since it is written: 'And there is nothing new under the sun,' which means that everything was settled at the time of the creation of the world?" Rav Yehuda said, "It is written, 'under the sun.' But 'above the sun' new things can take place." Rav Yosi asked, "Why does the Holy One have to make an announcement, since Rav Chizkiyah said that Rav Chiya said that at exactly the time a man is born and emerges in the world, his spouse is assigned to him?"

346. וְתָא חֲזֵי, בְּכָל אִינוּן דְּיוּקְנִין דְּנִשְׁמָתִין דְּעָלְמָא. כֻּלְּהוּ זוּגִין זוּגִין קַמֵּיהּ, לְבָתַר, כַּד אַתְיָין לְהַאי עָלְמָא, קֻדְשָׁא בְּרִיךְ הוּא מְזַוֵּוג זוּגִין. אָמַר ר' יִצְחָק, קוּדְשָׁא בְּרִיךְ הוּא אֲמַר בַּת פְּלוֹנִי לִפְלוֹנִי.

347. אָמַר רִבִּי יוֹסֵי, מַאי קָא מַיְירֵי, וְהָא כְּתִיב אֵין כָּל וְחָדָשׁ תַּחַת הַשָּׁמֶשׁ. אָמַר ר' יְהוּדָה, תַּחַת הַשָּׁמֶשׁ כְּתִיב, שֶׁאֲנִי לְעֵילָא. אָמַר רִבִּי יוֹסֵי, מַאי כְּרוֹזָא הָכָא, וְהָא אֲמַר ר' חִזְקִיָּה אֲמַר רִבִּי חִיָּיא, בְּהַהִיא שַׁעֲתָא מַמָּשׁ, דְּנָפִיק בַּר נָשׁ לְעָלְמָא, בַּת זוּגוֹ אוֹזְדַמְּנַת לוֹ.

Rav Aba responded, "Happy are the righteous, whose souls are adorned as they appear before the Holy One, before coming to this world. Because we have learned that when the Holy One, blessed be He, sends the souls forth to the world, all of these spirits and souls include a male and a female joined together.

"They are handed over to a minister, who is an emissary in charge of human conception and whose name is *Lailah*. So when the souls descend to the world and are handed over to that minister, they are separated from each other. Sometimes one precedes the other in coming down and entering the body of a human being.

"When their time to be married arrives, the Holy One, blessed be He, who knows these spirits and souls, joins them as they were before they came down to the world. And He announces, 'The daughter of this man shall go with the son of that man.'

348. אָמַר רִבִּי אַבָּא, זַכָּאִין אִינּוּן צַדִּיקַיָּא, דְּנִשְׁמַתְהוֹן מִתְעַטְּרִין קַמֵּי מַלְכָּא קַדִּישָׁא, עַד לָא יֵיתוּן לְעָלְמָא, דְּהָכֵי תָּנֵינָן, בְּהַהִיא שַׁעֲתָא דְּאַפִּיק קֻדְשָׁא בְּרִיךְ הוּא נִשְׁמָתִין לְעָלְמָא, כָּל אִינּוּן רוּחִין וְנִשְׁמָתִין, כֻּלְּהוּ כְּלִילָן דְּכַר וְנוּקְבָא, דְּמִתְחַבְּרָן כַּחֲדָא.

349. וְאִתְמַסְרָן בִּידָא דְּהַהוּא מְמַנָּא, שְׁלִיחָא דְּאִתְפַּקַּד עַל עִדּוּאֵיהוֹן דִּבְנֵי נָשָׁא, וְלַיְלָה שְׁמֵיהּ. וּבְשַׁעֲתָא דְּנַחְתִּין וְאִתְמַסְרָן בִּידוֹי, מִתְפָּרְשִׁין. וּלְזִמְנִין דָּא אַקְדִּים מִן דָּא, וְאָזֵוית לְהוּ בִּבְנֵי נָשָׁא.

350. וְכַד מָטָא עִידָן דְּזִוּוּגָא דִּלְהוֹן, קֻדְשָׁא בְּרִיךְ הוּא דְּיָדַע אִינּוּן רוּחִין וְנִשְׁמָתִין, מְחַבֵּר לוֹן כְּדְבְקַדְמֵיתָא, וּמַכְרִזָא עֲלַיְיהוּ.

"When they are joined together, they become one body and one soul, the right and left in proper unity. And because of this, 'there is nothing new under the sun.' This is nothing new, but rather a return to how they were before coming down to this world. Since only the Holy One, blessed be He, knows this, He therefore makes an announcement regarding them.

וְכַד אִתְחַזְּבְרָן, אִתְעֲבִידוּ חַד גּוּפָא וְחַד נִשְׁמָתָא, יְמִינָא וּשְׂמָאלָא כְּדְקָא חֲזֵי. וּבְגִין כָּךְ אֵין כָּל חָדָשׁ תַּחַת הַשָּׁמֶשׁ.

"You might say, 'But we have learned that a man obtains a mate according to his deeds and ways of behavior!' It is assuredly so! If he is meritorious and his ways are correct, then he deserves his own soulmate—to join her as when they left the Upper World."

351. וְאִי תֵּימָא הָא תָּנֵינָן, לֵית זַוּוּגָא, אֶלָּא לְפוּם עוֹבָדוֹי וְאָרְחוֹי דְּבַר נָשׁ. הָכֵי הוּא וַדַּאי, דְּאִי זָכֵי, וְעוֹבָדוֹי אִתְכַּשְׁרָן, זָכֵי לְהַהוּא דִּילֵיהּ, לְאִתְחַזְּבְרָא בֵּיהּ, כְּמָה דְנָפֵיק.

MEDITATION

Even after you've found your soul mate, there may be times when you feel as if you two are growing apart. A soul mate relationship isn't necessarily one in which you feel calm and peaceful all the time. It's not a matter of "I'm okay, you're okay." The ultimate purpose is constant spiritual growth. It is when that growth is occurring that the unity between the souls deepens.

This meditation can help bring your soul mate into your life. It can also strengthen your connection with a soul mate you have already found. Whenever you are awakened to desire for your soul mate—or whenever you need to renew your bond—use the meditation below.

דְּאִי זָכֵי, וְעוֹבָדוֹי אִתְכַּשְׁרָן, זָכֵי לְהַהוּא
lehahu zachei itkashran ve'ovadoi zachei de'i

דִּילֵיהּ, לְאִתְחַבְּרָא בֵּיהּ, כְּמָה דְּנָפֵיק
denateik kemah beih le'itchabara dileih

If he is meritorious and his ways are correct, then he deserves his own soul mate—to join her as when they left the Upper World.

STARTING SOMETHING NEW:

"BRINGING IN THE LIGHT"

(ZOHAR, BERESHEET B, VERSE 438)

We experience excitement and energy when we begin something new—but as time goes on, often the energy fades. The Zohar explains that we can sustain the power of our beginnings by bringing in the Creator's Light at the outset. As a tree depends on a seed, all future manifestations depend on their beginnings. What's more, all the moments of our lives, even those that seem to represent completion, are beginnings as well.

Kabbalah teaches that the true destination of all our journeys is complete joy and fulfillment. To reach this destination, we need connection with the Light. The Zohar explains that the Light we draw is referred to as the *Shechinah*, the female aspect of the Creator, which is there to assist us and protect us in any journey we take.

This section reveals the importance of bringing the Light into all our beginnings—that is, into everything we do, we should always be accompanied by the Light.

Rav Shimon was traveling, accompanied by his son, Rav Elazar, Rav Yosi, and Rav Chiya. Rav Elazar said to his father: "The road is clear before us, and we would like to hear words of wisdom."

438. רַבִּי שִׁמְעוֹן הֲוָה אָזִיל בְּאָרְחָא, וַהֲווֹ עִמֵּיהּ רַבִּי אֶלְעָזָר בְּרֵיהּ, וְרַבִּי יוֹסֵי, וְרַבִּי חִיָּיא. עַד דַּהֲוָה אָזִיל, אָמַר רַבִּי אֶלְעָזָר לַאֲבוּהִי, אָרְחָא מִתְתַּקְּנָא קָמָן, בָּעֵינָן לְמִשְׁמַע מִלֵּי דְאוֹרַיְיתָא.

Rav Shimon began to speak of the words: "Even when a fool walks on his way, his heart is lacking." Rav Shimon said, "When a man is on a journey and he wishes to make his ways agreeable to the Creator, he should consult the Creator and pray to Him before he proceeds, so that his journey will be ensured. This is as we have learned regarding the verse, 'Righteousness goes before him then he shall set his feet on his way,' which means that he should pray that the *Shechinah* should not part from him."

439. פָּתַח רַבִּי שִׁמְעוֹן וְאָמַר, גַּם בַּדֶּרֶךְ כְּשֶׁהַסָּכָל הֹלֵךְ לִבּוֹ חָסֵר וְגוֹ'. כַּד בַּ"נ בָּעֵי לְאַתְקְנָא אָרְחֵיהּ קָמֵי קֻדְשָׁא בְּרִיךְ הוּא. עַד לָא יִפּוֹק לְאָרְחָא, בָּעֵי לְאִמְלָכָא בֵּיהּ, וּלְצַלֵּי קָמֵיהּ עַל אָרְחֵיהּ. כְּמָה דְתָנִינָן, דִּכְתִיב צֶדֶק לְפָנָיו יְהַלֵּךְ וְיָשֵׂם לְדֶרֶךְ פְּעָמָיו. דְּהָא שְׁכִינְתָּא לָא אִתְפָּרְשָׁא מִנֵּיהּ.

Of him who has no faith in his master, it is written: "Even when a fool walks on his way, his heart is lacking." Rav Shimon asked, "What is meant by "his heart?" "It

440. וּמָאן דְּאִיהוּ לָא מְהֵימְנָא בְּמָרֵיהּ, מַה כְּתִיב בֵּיהּ, וְגַם בַּדֶּרֶךְ כְּשֶׁהַסָּכָל הֹלֵךְ לִבּוֹ חָסֵר, מַאן לִבּוֹ,

is the Holy One, blessed be He, whose *Shechinah* does not accompany fools. Thus, 'his heart is lacking' means that the fool lacks His aid along the way. This is all because a man who does not trust in his Master does not seek help from his Master before he starts his journey.

דָּא קֻדְשָׁא בְּרִיךְ הוּא, דְּלָא יָהַךְ עֲמֵיהּ בְּאָרְחָא, וְגָרַע מִן סִיַּיעְתֵּיהּ בְּאָרְחֵיהּ. בְּגִין דְּהַהוּא בַּר נָשׁ, דְּלָא מְהֵימָן בֵּיהּ בְּמָארֵיהּ, עַד לָא יִפּוֹק בְּאָרְחָא, לָא בָּעֵי סִיַּעְתָּא דְּמָארֵיהּ.

"And even when he is on his way, he is not occupied with the study of wisdom, and thus 'his heart is lacking.' Because he does not follow his Master, His Master is not found on his way. The verse continues: 'And he proclaims to all that he is foolish,' meaning that even when he hears words of true faith in God, he says that it is foolish to pay attention."

441. וַאֲפִילוּ בְּאָרְחָא, כַּד אִיהוּ אָזִיל, לָא אִשְׁתַּדַּל בְּמִלֵּי דְּאוֹרַיְיתָא. וּבְגִינֵי כָּךְ, לִבּוֹ חָסֵר, דְּלָא אָזִיל בַּהֲדֵיהּ דְּמָרֵיהּ, וְלָא אִשְׁתְּכַח בְּאָרְחֵיהּ. וְאָמַר לַכֹּל סָכָל הוּא. אֲפִילוּ כַּד שָׁמַע מִלָּה דִּמְהֵימְנוּתָא דְּמָארֵיהּ, הוּא אָמַר, דְּטִפְּשׁוּתָא הוּא, לְאִשְׁתַּדָּלָא בֵּיהּ.

75

MEDITATION

Whenever you are beginning an endeavor or a new relationship, use this meditation to bring the *Shechinah* into your journey, and to gain and sustain the blessings that the Light brings.

כַּד ב"נ בָּעֵי לְאַתְקָנָא אָרְחֵיה קַמֵּי קֻדְשָׁא
kudsha kamei archeih le'atkana ba'ei barnash kad

בְּרִיךְ הוּא. עַד לָא יִפּוֹק לְאָרְחָא, בָּעֵי לְאַמְלָכָא
le'amlacha ba'ei le'archa yipok la ad hu berich

בֵּיהּ, וּלְצַלֵּי קַמֵּיהּ עַל אָרְחֵיהּ.
archei al kameih uletzalei bei

Rav Shimon said, "When a man is on a journey and he wishes to make his ways agreeable to the Creator, he should consult the Creator and pray to Him before he proceeds, so that his journey will be ensured."

R EPLACING   D OUBT   WITH

C ERTAINTY :

"H ER   HUSBAND   IS   KNOWN   IN   THE   GATES"

(Z OHAR ,   V AYERA ,   VERSE   151)

While life certainly includes key turning points and dramatic
moments, our most important endeavors usually take years
rather than minutes or hours. Whether it's building your
career, or raising a family, or dealing with a difficult health
issue, this section—one of the most important in the entire
Zohar—reveals the single most basic element you need to connect with the Light. That element is *certainty.*

Certainty is the power that draws the Light into our lives.
Certainty is the Vessel into which the Light flows. Just as quan-
tum physics tells us the process of observation creates what is
observed, the Light of the Creator becomes present in our lives
to the degree that we have certainty of its presence. And the
reverse of this is also true: To the degree that we doubt the existence of the Light, then to that degree the Light literally does
not exist in our lives.

This is an amazing lesson. Consciousness is the key. It is our
consciousness that literally brings the Creator into our lives. In
this passage, the fact that consciousness fosters the Creator's
presence is expressed through the double meaning of the
Hebrew word for "gates." In Hebrew, "gates" (*she'arim*) also
connotes to "reveal" or "construe" (*mesha'er*). The Zohar

explains that in the verse, "Her husband is known in the gates," there is a deeper meaning: God is known and revealed to the extent that our own consciousness sees the Light.

Rav Yehuda spoke of the verse: "'Her husband is known in the gates, when he sits among the elders of the land.' Come and behold: the Creator is exalted in His glory, because He is hidden and greatly elevated. Since the creation of the world, nobody has ever been able to grasp and conceive His entire wisdom. No one is able to comprehend it.

"He is concealed and exalted high above the reach of both lower and supernal beings. He is so far above that they all proclaim: 'Blessed be the glory of God from His place.' The people on earth proclaim that God is high above, as it is written: 'His glory is above the heavens,' but the angels say that God is down below, as it is written: 'His glory is over all the earth.' Thus, both supernal and human beings declare: 'Blessed be the glory of God from His place,' because He is unknowable, and no one is able to grasp Him. Thus, how does one explain the verse: 'Her husband is known in the gates?'

151. ר' יְהוּדָה פָּתַח, נוֹדַע בַּשְּׁעָרִים בַּעְלָהּ בְּשִׁבְתּוֹ עִם זִקְנֵי אָרֶץ. תָּא חֲזֵי קוּדְשָׁא בְּרִיךְ הוּא אִסְתַּלַּק בִּיקָרֵיהּ, דְּאִיהוּ גָּנִיז וְסָתִים, בְּעִלּוּיָא סַגִּיא. לָאו אִיהֵי בְּעָלְמָא, וְלָא הֲוָה מִן יוֹמָא דְּאִתְבְּרֵי עָלְמָא, דְּיָכִיל לְקַיְּימָא עַל וְחָכְמְתָא דִילֵיהּ, וְלָא יָכִיל לְקַיְּימָא בֵּיהּ.

152. בְּגִין דְּאִיהוּ גָּנִיז וְסָתִים, וְאִסְתַּלַּק לְעֵילָא לְעֵילָא, וְכֻלְּהוּ עִלָּאֵי וְתַתָּאֵי לָא יָכְלִין לְאִתְדַּבְּקָא, עַד דְּכֻלְּהוּ אַמְרִין בָּרוּךְ כְּבוֹד ה' מִמְּקוֹמוֹ. תַּתָּאֵי אַמְרֵי דְּאִיהוּ לְעֵילָא, דִּכְתִיב עַל הַשָּׁמַיִם כְּבוֹדוֹ. עִלָּאֵי אַמְרֵי דְּאִיהוּ לְתַתָּא, דִּכְתִיב עַל כָּל הָאָרֶץ כְּבוֹדֶךָ. עַד דְּכֻלְּהוּ עִלָּאֵי וְתַתָּאֵי, אַמְרֵי בָּרוּךְ כְּבוֹד ה' מִמְּקוֹמוֹ. בְּגִין דְּלָא אִתְיְידַע, וְלָא הֲוָה מַאן דְּיָכִיל לְקַיְּימָא בֵּיהּ, וְאַתְּ אַמְרַתְּ נוֹדַע בַּשְּׁעָרִים בַּעְלָהּ.

"Most certainly, 'Her husband is known in the gates' refers to the Creator, who is known and conceived according to what each one of us construes in his mind and is able to grasp with the Spirit of Wisdom. Thus, he is able to understand according to what he is able to assume. Therefore, it is written: 'Her husband is known in the gates,' although full knowledge of Him is far beyond the reach of anyone."

153. אֶלָּא וַדַּאי, נוֹדָע בַּשְּׁעָרִים בַּעְלָהּ. דָּא קוּדְשָׁא בְּרִיךְ הוּא. דְּאִיהוּ אִתְיְדַע וְאִתְדַּבַּק, לְפוּם מַה דִּמְשַׁעֵר בְּלִבֵּיהּ, כָּל חַד וְחַד, כַּמָה דְּיָכִיל לְאַדְבְּקָא בְּרוּחָא דְּחָכְמְתָא. וּלְפוּם מַה דִּמְשַׁעֵר בְּלִבֵּיהּ, הָכִי אִתְיְדַע בְּלִבֵּיהּ. וּבְגִינֵי כָּךְ, נוֹדָע בַּשְּׁעָרִים, בְּאִינּוּן שְׁעָרִים. אֲבָל דְּאִתְיְדַע כְּדְקָא יֵאוּת, לָא הֲוָה מַאן דְּיָכִיל לְאַדְבְּקָא וּלְמִנְדַּע לֵיהּ.

MEDITATION

When you feel the need for certainty to manifest the greatest possible Light in your work, your relationships, or in any area of your life in which you feel a lack, use this meditation to draw the maximum amount of blessings from the Light of the Creator. Use it also before undertaking any important spiritual action, to strengthen certainty in your abilities and in the blessings you will draw.

אֶלָּא וַדַּאי, נוֹדַע בַּשְׁעָרִים בַּעְלָהּ. דָּא קוּדְשָׁא
kudsha da ba'alah bashe'arim noda vadayi ela

בְּרִיךְ הוּא. דְּאִיהוּ אִתְיְדַע וְאִתְדַּבַּק, לְפוּם מַה
mah kefum ve'itdabak ityeda dehihu hu berich

דִּמְשַׁעֵר בְּלִבֵּיהּ, כָּל חַד, כַּמָּה דְּיָכִיל
deyachil kamah chad kol belibeih dimsha'er

לְאִתְדַּבְּקָא בְּרוּחָא דְּחָכְמְתָא.
dechochmeta berucha leidbeka

Most certainly, 'Her husband is known in the gates' refers to the Creator, who is known and conceived according to what each one of us construes in his mind and is able to grasp with the Spirit of Wisdom.

DESIRING MORE, AND NOT SETTLING FOR LESS:

"THE CONCEALED BOOK"

(ZOHAR, SAFRA DETZNIUTA, VERSE 1)

Many people reach a point in their lives in which they're not completely satisfied or fulfilled, so they conclude that life was never *meant* to be completely fulfilling. They resign themselves to settling for something less. But Kabbalah teaches that this is the exact opposite of the truth. We should never settle for less than total fulfillment, both physically and spiritually.

One of the greatest dangers to our spiritual work is thinking that we've achieved a certain level of development, and there's no need to delve deeper. The Zohar tells us that we should want more than we've ever imagined, and that the Light will bring it into our lives. Our purpose in this world is to have total and complete joy and fulfillment. To bring about that purpose, our deepest yearning should be for a connection with the Creator's Light.

But as the parable in this section explains, connection with the Light means continuous striving and yearning for deeper wisdom. Rav Shimon explains that without constant growth in understanding, there will not be a constantly growing revelation of the Creator's Light.

To truly yearn for deeper understanding is much more than an intellectual experience. In a letter to Rav Berg, my father and teacher, from Rav Yehuda Brandwein, his teacher/master, Rav Brandwein referred to the fact that there are infinite levels of wisdom in every teaching. Discovering these levels is a physical, sensory experience—like finding a new taste in a sip of wine. We can't discover the next revelation unless our eagerness for it is always present. As long as our desire for understanding continuously grows, our taste and feel for the wisdom will continuously deepen. We are able to physically sense the Light of the Creator within.

This reading is an introduction to a section of the Zohar called "The Concealed Book" (*Safra Detzniuta*), which contains the foundation for all the secrets. Rav Shimon explains the need for deeper learning, even beyond the foundations.

What is the Concealed Book? Rav Shimon said, "There are five chapters, contained in a great chamber, which fill the entire earth." Rav Yehuda said, "If these include the entire wisdom, they are the best and there is no need to study further." Rav Shimon said, "This is true for one who has entered Wisdom and came out from it in peace. But it is not so for one who did not enter Wisdom and emerge from it in peace.

1. מַאן צְנִיעוּתָא דְּסִפְרָא.
אֲמַר רִבִּי שִׁמְעוֹן, וַחֲמִשָׁה
פִּרְקִין אִינּוּן דִּכְלִילָן בְּהֵיכַל
רַב, וּמַלְיָין כָּל אַרְעָא. אֲמַר ר
יְהוּדָה, אִי כְּלִילָן הֲנֵי, מִכֻּלְּהוּ
עֲדִיפֵי. אֲמַר ר שִׁמְעוֹן, הָכִי
הוּא, לְמַאן דְּעָאל וְנָפַק,
וּלְמַאן דְּלָא עָאל וְנָפַק לָאו
הָכִי.

This is likened to a man who lived in the mountains and was not acquainted with the city inhabitants. He sowed wheat, and then he ate the wheat just as it was. One day, he came to the city, where he was served with good bread. That person said, 'What is this?' They answered him, 'This is bread to be eaten.' He ate and it was delicious to his palate. He said, 'What is this made from?' They said, 'It is made from wheat.' Afterwards, they served him cookies mixed with oil. He tasted them. He asked,

2. מַתְלָא, לְבַר נָשׁ דַּהֲוָה
דַּיּוּרֵיהּ בֵּינֵי טוּרִין, וְלָא יָדַע
בְּדִיּוּרֵי מָתָא. זָרַע וְחִטִּין.
וְאָכִיל וְחִטֵי בְּגוּפַיְיהוּ. יוֹמָא חַד
עָאל לְמָתָא, אַקְרִיבוּ לֵיהּ
נַהֲמָא טָבָא. אֲמַר הַהוּא בַּר
נָשׁ, דְּנָא לְמָה. אָמְרוּ נַהֲמָא
הוּא לְמֵיכַל. אָכַל וְטָעַם
לְוָדָא לְוַחֵכֵיהּ. אֲמַר וּמִמַּה
אִתְעֲבֵיד דָּא. אֲמְרוּ מֵחִטִּין.
לְבָתַר אַקְרִיבוּ לֵיהּ גְּרִיצִין
דְּלִישִׁין בְּמִשְׁחָא. טָעַם מִנַּיְיהוּ,
אֲמַר וְאִלֵּין מִמַּה אִתְעֲבִידוּ.
אֲמְרוּ מֵחִטִּין.

'And what are these made from?' They answered, 'From wheat.' Afterwards, they offered him food fit for kings kneaded with oil and honey. He said, 'What are these made from?' They told him, 'From wheat'. He said, 'I certainly have all these, because I eat the essence of all these, which is wheat.' Because of this opinion, he did not learn how to make all these delicacies and he did not know of the delights of the world — thus, they were lost to him. It is also so with one who grasps the generality of wisdom, but does not know the delights and delicacies that are derived from that generality.

לְבָתַר אַקְרִיבוּ לֵיהּ טְרִיקֵי מַלְכִין, דְּלִישִׁין בְּדוּבְשָׁא וּמִשְׁחָא. אָמַר וְאִלֵּין מִמַּה אִתְעֲבִידוּ. אֲמָרוּ מֵחִטִּין. אָמַר וַדַּאי אֲנָא מָארֵי דְּכָל אִלֵּין, דַּאֲנָא אָכִיל עִקָּרָא דְּכָל אִלֵּין דְּאִיהוּ וְחִטָּה. בְּגִין הַהוּא דַעְתָּא מֵעֲדוּנֵי עָלְמָא לָא יָדַע וְאִתְאֲבִידוּ מִנֵּיהּ. כַּךְ, מַאן דְּנָקִיט כְּלָלָא, וְלָא יָדַע בְּכֻלְּהוּ עֲדוּנִין דִּמְהַנְיָין, דְּנַפְקִין מֵהַהוּא כְּלָלָא.

MEDITATION

This meditation awakens desire for more in every area of life—as well as the understanding that there always is more. It brings consciousness of the need to continually deepen your fulfillment from life and your grasp of spiritual wisdom—to never be satisfied with your present situation.

כַּךְ, מַאן דְּנָקִיט כְּלָלָא, וְלֹא יָדַע בְּכֻלְהוּ
bechulhu   yada   vela   kelala   denakit   ma'an   kach

עֵדוּנִין דִּמְהַנְיָן, דְּנַפְקִין מֵהַהוּא כְּלָלָא.
kelala   mehahu   denafkin   dimhanyan   idonin

It is also so with one who grasps the generality of wisdom, but does not know the delights and delicacies that are derived from that generality.

Drawing in Miracles:

"The wife of Obadiah"

(Zohar, Lech Lecha, verse 261)

Sometimes we feel like there is no hope. There seems to be no way out, short of a miracle. Yet as the Zohar explains, the consciousness of despair is exactly what prevents miracles from taking place. For something to happen that will break through the limits of the natural, normal—that's what a miracle is, after all—there needs to be a starting point for the miracle to rest upon.

When a doctor tells a patient there is only a five percent chance for survival, the patient should cling to that five percent chance. In the same way, someone who has only a small amount of money should use that money in asking the Creator to bring a miracle. The money will provide a place for the miracle to come and rest. No matter how small it may be—whether it's a physical object or a point in consciousness—this can be the space upon which miracles can come to rest.

To explain this, the Zohar draws upon the biblical story of the wife of Obadiah, who found herself deeply in debt after her husband's death (2 Kings 4:2). When creditors threatened to take her sons into slavery, she went to the prophet Elisha for help. Perhaps surprisingly, the prophet simply asked, "What do you have in your house?" When the woman replied that she had only a small vessel filled with a little oil, Elisha told her to borrow additional vessels from her neighbors. She did so, and as Elisha directed, she poured the oil from her vessel into the new ones. Miraculously, the widow was able to fill all the vessels from the contents of her own.

Regarding this story, the kabbalists asked a simple question: If the prophet had the power to perform a miracle on behalf of this widow, why was it important for him to know what was in her house? Why was it necessary for her to have a small amount of oil for the miracle to occur? The answer is illuminating. First, there needed to be a starting point for the miracle, which was the small amount of oil the widow began with. Once that was found to be present, it could miraculously transform from scarcity to abundance.

Like the widow in the biblical story, we may feel despair. We hope that somehow the Creator will help us through with a miracle—but we ourselves have to create a place for that miracle to come into our lives. If we don't already have such a place, we need to create one. Once we create a place, however small, then the miracle can occur.

Rav Yehuda opened the discourse by quoting the verse: "I am my beloved's, and his desire is toward me." This means that an awakening below results in an awakening above. There can be no awakening from above until there is an awakening from below. Blessings from above will rest in a place of substance not in an empty space.

We know this from the wife of Obadiah, to whom Elisha said: "Tell me, what have you in the house." He asked this because blessings from above do not rest on an empty table, nor in an empty place. She replied, "Your handmaid has nothing in the house but a vessel of oil." Regarding this, Rav Yehuda asked: "How much was in the vessel? There was only enough oil to smear the little finger."

Elisha said, "You have reassured me. I did not know how the blessings of above would rest in an empty place. But now that you have some oil, this is the place where the blessings shall rest."

261. אַזַר הַדְּבָרִים הָאֵלֶּה הָיָה דְּבַר ה' אֶל אַבְרָם וגו'. ר' יְהוּדָה פָּתַח אֲנִי לְדוֹדִי וְעָלַי תְּשׁוּקָתוֹ. הָא אוּקְמוּהָ, אֲבָל בְּאִתְעֲרוּתָא דִלְתַתָּא, אִשְׁתְּכַח אִתְעֲרוּתָא לְעֵילָא, דְּהָא לָא אִתְעַר לְעֵילָא. עַד דְּאִתְעַר לְתַתָּא. וּבִרְכָאן דִלְעֵילָא לָא מִשְׁתַּכְּחֵי, אֶלָּא בַּמֶּה דְּאִית בֵּיה מַמָּשָׁא, וְלָא אִיהוּ רֵיקָנָא.

262. מְנָלָן. מֵאֲשֵׁת עוֹבַדְיָהוּ, דְּאָמַר לָהּ אֱלִישָׁע הַגִּידִי לִי מַה יֶּשׁ לָךְ בַּבָּיִת, דְּהָא בִּרְכָאן דִלְעֵילָא, לָא שָׁרְיָין עַל פָּתוֹרָא רֵיקָנָא, וְלָא בַּאֲתַר רֵיקָנָא. מַה כְּתִיב, וַתֹּאמֶר אֵין לְשִׁפְחָתְךָ כֹל בַּבַּיִת כִּי אִם אָסוּךְ שָׁמֶן. מַאי אָסוּךְ. אֶלָּא אָמַר לוֹ, שִׁעוּרָא דְּהַאי מִשְׁחָא, לָאו אִיהִי, אֶלָּא כְּדֵי מִשְׁיַחַת אֶצְבְּעָא זְעֵירָא.

263. אָמַר לָהּ, נְחַמְתַּנִי. דְּהָא לָא יְדַעְנָא, הֵיאַךְ יִשְׁרוֹן בִּרְכָאן דִלְעֵילָא, בְּדוּכְתָּא רֵיקָנָא, אֲבָל הַשְׁתָּא דְּאִית לָךְ שֶׁמֶן, דָּא הוּא אֲתַר, לְאִשְׁתַּכְּחָא בֵּיה בִּרְכָאן. מְנָלָן דִּכְתִיב כַּשֶּׁמֶן הַטּוֹב וגו'. וְסֵיפֵיהּ מַה כְּתִיב, כִּי שָׁם צִוָּה ה' אֶת הַבְּרָכָה חַיִּים עַד הָעוֹלָם. וּבְאַתְרָא דָּא שָׁרָאן בִּרְכָאן.

MEDITATION

In times of challenge, this meditation gives us the power to discover a place—or to create a place—in which miracles can occur.

וּבִרְכָאן דִּלְעֵילָא לָא מִשְׁתַּכְּחֵי, אֶלָּא בַּמֶּה
bameh ela mishtakchei la dile'eila uvirchan

דְּאִית בֵּיהּ מַמָּשָׁא, וְלָאו אִיהוּ רֵיקַנְיָא
reikanya ihu velo mamasha beih de'it

Blessings from above rest in a place of substance, not in an empty space.

TRANSFORMING GRIEF:

"THE PASSING OF THE THREE FRIENDS"

(ZOHAR, IDRA RABA, VERSE 353)

There are times in life when we are genuinely saddened. It may be because of death, loss, or just that someone has done or said something to hurt us. In this section, the Zohar shows us that even great souls such as Rav Aba experienced moments of sadness. But although sadness is part of being human, sadness also ends once we see the bigger picture.

The souls of Rav Yosi, Rav Chizkiyah, and Rav Yesa, three of the friends, left this world immediately after the Idra Raba (the Great Assembly) and its immense revelation of Light. Why did their passing take place at this time? A supernal voice explains to Rav Shimon that their deaths were absolutely not a punishment for them, but were indeed great blessings. They had completed their work and were ready to ascend.

Rav Aba, however, remains saddened—until he experiences a vision of the three friends in the World to Come. At first he could see only what man revealed in the physical dimension. When he saw the complete picture of his friends' happiness, his sadness was transformed to joy.

During the Idra Raba, Rav Shimon revealed secrets that had never before been disclosed. In fact, this revelation brought a greater volume of Light into the world than at any time since the revelation at Mount Sinai.

We have learned that before the departure of the friends from the Idra Raba (the Great Assembly), Rav Yosi, son of Rav Yaakov; Rav Chizkiyah; and Rav Yesa died. The friends saw that holy angels carried them aloft in a veil. The friends became calm and were silent as Rav Shimon spoke. He cried out: "Perhaps, heaven forbid, a writ was decreed for us to be punished, since it was revealed through us what has not been revealed since the day Moses stood on Mount Sinai. It is written: 'And he was there with God forty days and forty nights...' What have I done, if this is the reason for their punishment?"

He heard a voice say: "Rav Shimon, you deserve praise. Praised is your lot and the lot of your friends who live with you, since it was revealed to you what has not been revealed to all the legions above. However, come and see that it is written: 'He shall lay its foundation with his firstborn,

353. תָּנָא, עַד לָא נַפְקוּ
וַחַבְרַיָיא מֵהַהוּא אִדְרָא, מִיתוּ
ר' יוֹסֵי בַּר' יַעֲקֹב, וְר' וְחִזְקִיָּה,
וְר' יֵיסָא. וְחָזוּ וְחַבְרַיָיא, דַּהֲווֹ
נַטְלִין לוֹן מַלְאָכִין קַדִּישִׁין
בְּהַהוּא פָּרְסָא. וְאר"ע מִלָּה,
וְאִשְׁתְּכְכוּ. צָווַח וְאָמַר, שֶׁמָּא
ח"ו גְּזֵרָה אִתְגְּזַר עֲלָנָא
לְאִתְעַנְּשָׁא, דְּאִתְגְּלֵי עַל יְדָנָא,
מַה דְּלָא אִתְגְּלֵי מִיּוֹמָא
דְּקָאִים מֹשֶׁה עַל טוּרָא דְּסִינַי,
דִּכְתִיב וַיְהִי שָׁם עִם יְיָ
אַרְבָּעִים יוֹם וְאַרְבָּעִים לַיְלָה
וְגוֹ'. מַה אֲנָא הָכָא. אִי בְּגִין
דָּא אִתְעַנָּשׁוּ.

354. שָׁמַע קָלָא, זַכָּאָה אַנְתְּ
ר'ע, זַכָּאָה וְחוּלָקָךְ וְחַבְרַיָיא,
אִלֵּין דְּקָיְימִין בַּהֲדָךְ, דְּהָא
אִתְגְּלֵי לְכוֹן מַה דְּלָא אִתְגְּלֵי
לְכָל חֵילָא דִּלְעֵילָא, אֲבָל
ת"ח, דְּהָא כְּתִיב, בִּבְכוֹרוֹ
יְיַסְּדֶנָּה וּבִצְעִירוֹ יַצִּיב דְּלָתֶיהָ.
וכ"ע דְּבִרְעוּ סַגִּי וְתַקִּיף,
אִתְדָּבְקוּ נַפְשַׁתְהוֹן בְּשַׁעֲתָא
דָּא דְּאִתְנְסִיבוּ.

and with his youngest son shall he set up the gates of it.' Certainly, the souls of the friends were joined with a great strong, passion at the time they were taken by the angels. Praised is their lot that, through perfection, they passed away."

זַכָּאָה וזולְקֵהוֹן, דְּהָא בִּשְׁלֵימוּתָא אִסְתָּלָקוּ.

We have learned that while these secrets were revealed, all those in the Upper and Lower Worlds trembled with excitement. A voice was awakened and declared, in 250 supernal worlds, that ancient secrets were being revealed below. During the Idra Raba, while these three friends were perfuming and perfecting their souls, their souls departed this world with a kiss and were attached to the supernal veil. The uppermost angels took them and raised them above.

355. תָּאנָא, בְּעוֹד דְּאִתְגַּלְיָין מִלִּין, אִתְרְגִישׁוּ עִלָּאִין וְתַתָּאִין, וְקָלָא אִתְּעַר בְּמָאתָן וַחֲמִשִׁין עָלְמִין דְּהָא מִלִּין עַתִּיקִין לְתַתָּא אִתְגַּלְיָין, וְעַד דְּאִלֵּין מִתְבַּסְּמָן נִשְׁמָתַיְיהוּ בְּאִינּוּן מִלִּין, נַפְקָא נִשְׁמָתַיְיהוּ בִּנְשִׁיקָה, וְאִתְקְשַׁר בְּהַהוּא פַּרְסָא, וְנַטְלִין לְהוֹ מַלְאֲכֵי עִלָּאֵי, וְסַלְקִין לוֹן לְעֵילָא. וַאֲמַאי אִלֵּין. מִשּׁוּם דְּעָאלָן וְלָא נַפְקוּ זִמְנָא אַחֲרָא מִן קַדְמַת דְּנָא, וְכֻלְּהוֹ אַחֲרָנֵי עָאלוּ וְנַפְקוּ.

Rav Shimon said, "How happy is the lot of these three, and because of this, praised is our lot in the World to Come."

356. אר"ע, כַּמָּה זַכָּאָה וזולְקֵהוֹן דְּהָנֵי תְּלָתָא, וְזַכָּאָה וזולְקָנָא לְעָלְמָא דְּאָתֵי, בְּגִין דָּא.

A second voice sounded and said: "But you that did cleave to God are alive every one of you this day." They rose and departed. Everywhere the seven looked, fragrances were ascending. Rav Shimon said, "It seems from this that the world receives blessings because of us." All their faces were shining bright and the people of the world could not look at them.

נָפַק קָלָא תִּנְיָינוּת וְאָמַר, וְאַתֶּם הַדְּבֵקִים בַּיְיָ אֱלֹהֵיכֶם חַיִּים כֻּלְּכֶם הַיּוֹם. קָמוּ וְאָזְלוּ. בְּכָל אֲתָר דַּהֲווֹ מִסְתַּכְּלֵי סָלִיק רֵיחִין. אר"ש שָׁמַע מִינָּה, דִּלְעָלְמָא מִתְבְּרֵךְ בְּגִינָן. וַהֲווֹ נַהֲרִין אַנְפּוֹי דְּכֻלְּהוּ, וְלָא הֲווֹ יַכְלִין בְּנֵי עָלְמָא לְאִסְתַּכְּלָא בְּהוּ.

357. So we have learned that ten entered the Idra Raba, and seven left it. Rav Shimon rejoiced at this, but Rav Aba was saddened. One day, Rav Aba was sitting with Rav Shimon. Rav Shimon spoke. They saw the three departed friends. Upper angels were showing them the treasures and chambers above, that had been prepared for their honor. The angels were introducing them into the mountains of pure persimmon. Then Rav Aba's mind was calmed, and at peace.

357. תָּאנָא, עֲשָׂרָה עָאלוּ, וְשִׁבְעָא נַפְקוּ, וַהֲוָה חַדֵּי ר"ש. וְרִבִּי אַבָּא עָצִיב. יוֹמָא חַד הֲוָה יָתִיב ר"ש וְרִבִּי אַבָּא עַמֵּיהּ, אר"ש מִכָּה, וְחָזְמוּ לְאִלֵּין תְּלָתָא דַּהֲווֹ מַיְיתִין לְהוֹן מַלְאָכִין עִלָּאִין, וּמְחַזְּזֵין לְהוּ גְּנִיזִין וְאַדְרִין דִּלְעֵילָּא, בְּגִין יְקָרָא דִּלְהוֹן. וַהֲווֹ עַיְילֵי לוֹן בְּטוּרֵי דְּאַפַּרְסְמוֹנָא דַּכְיָא. נָח דַּעְתֵּיהּ דְּרִבִּי אַבָּא.

358. We have learned that from that day on, the friends did not leave the house of Rav Shimon. When Rav Shimon

358. תָּאנָא, מֵהַהוּא יוֹמָא לָא אַעְדוּ חַבְרַיָּיא מִבֵּי ר"ש.

was revealing secrets, no one else was present. Rav Shimon referred to them as: 'We are the seven eyes of God' as is written: "Those seven . . . the eyes of God." Rav Aba said to Rav Shimon: "We are six candles illuminated by the seventh. You are the seventh of each one, because the six cannot endure without the seventh, since everything is dependent on the seventh." Rav Yehuda used to refer to Rav Shimon as: "Shabbat, from which all six days get their blessing," as is written: 'Shabbat to God,' or 'Holy to God.' Just as Shabbat is holy to God, so is Rav Shimon holy Shabbat to God.

וְכַד הֲוָה ר'ע מְגַלֶּה רָזִין, לָא מִשְׁתַּכְחִין תַּמָּן אֶלָּא אִינוּן. וַהֲוָה קָאֲרִי לְהוֹ רִבִּי שִׁמְעוֹן, שִׁבְעָה אֲנָן עֵינֵי יְיָ. דִּכְתִיב, שִׁבְעָה אֵלֶּה עֵינֵי יְיָ וְעָלַן אִתְּמַר. א'ר אַבָּא, אֲנָן שִׁיתָא בּוּצִינֵי, דִּנְהַרָאן מִשְּׁבִיעָאָה. אַנְתְּ הוּא שְׁבִיעָאָה דְּכֻלָּא. דְּהָא לֵית קְיוּמָא לְשִׁיתָא, בַּר מִשְּׁבִיעָאָה. דְּכֹלָּא תָּלֵי בִּשְׁבִיעָאָה. רִבִּי יְהוּדָה קָאֲרֵי לֵיהּ שַׁבָּת, דְּכֻלְּהוּ שִׁיתָא מִנֵּיהּ מִתְבָּרְכִין, דִּכְתִיב שַׁבָּת לַיְיָ, קֹדֶשׁ לַיְיָ, מַה שַׁבָּת לַיְיָ קֹדֶשׁ, אוֹף ר'ע שַׁבָּת לַיְיָ קֹדֶשׁ.

MEDITATION

This meditation allows you to see sadness in a wider perspective. It brings awareness of the fact that a bigger picture exists, and that often the awareness alone is extremely helpful. This section goes even further, by opening us to an understanding of what the bigger picture includes: Everything is for good, even if it's not apparent in the moment.

יוֹמָא חַד הֲוָה יָתִיב ר"ש וְרִבִּי אַבָּא עִמֵּיהּ,
imeih Aba veRibbi Ribbi Shimon yativ havah chad yoma

אר"ש מִלָּה, וְחָמוּ לְאִלֵּין תְּלָתָא דַּהֲווֹ
dahavo tela'a leilein vechamu milah amar Ribbi Shimon

לְהוּ וּמְחַזְּיָן, עִלָּאִין מַלְאָכִין לְהוֹן מַיְיתִין
lehu umchazyan ila'in malachin lehon mayitin

דִּלְהוֹן. יְקָרָא בְּגִין דִּלְעֵילָא, וְאִדָּרִין גְּנִיזִין
dilhon yekara begin dileila ve'idarin genizin

דַּכְיָא. דַּאֲפַרְסְמוֹנָא בְּטוּרֵי לוֹן עַיְּילֵי וַהֲווֹ
dachya de'afarsmona beturei lon ay'lei vahavo

אַבָּא. דְּרִבִּי דַּעְתֵּיהּ נָח
Aba deRibbi da'ateih nach

One day, Rav Aba was sitting with Rav Shimon. Rav Shimon spoke. They saw the three departed friends. Upper angels were showing them the treasures and chambers above, that had been prepared for their honor. The angels were introducing them into the mountains of pure persimmon. Then Rav Aba's mind was calmed, and at peace.

96

II

MEDITATIONS
FOR SPIRITUAL
GROWTH

WHOLEHEARTED EFFORT AND INFINITE REWARD:

"THEY SHOULD BRING ME AN OFFERING"

(ZOHAR, TRUMAH, VERSE 34)

Often our spiritual actions don't bring about the fulfillment we expect. The Zohar tells us that the secret to receiving fulfillment and connection with the Light through our actions lies in performing those actions with effort and commitment. As the Zohar makes clear, anyone can merit a connection with the Light of the Creator, but when we perform actions that are intended to bring about that connection, we must extend ourselves physically as well as in the level of our investment. Only then will our actions bring about complete fulfillment and connection with the Light. It is not enough to simply perform spiritual actions. To merit connection with the Light, action must be done with wholehearted effort and complete commitment.

Rav Shimon began, "'They should bring Me an offering, from every man whose heart awakens him to give.' 'That they should bring Me' means that if someone wishes to undertake a precept—a positive action—and to aspire towards the Holy One, blessed be He, it is necessary that the person not strive halfheartedly and in vain; but rather he should make an effort with all his strength, according to his capacity. We have spoken about this in many places: and this is the correct way for a person to strive after the Holy One, blessed be He, as it is written: 'Every man shall give as he is able, according to the blessings your God has given you.'

"And if you ask, is it not written: 'Come and take, and eat; come, take wine and milk without money and without a price?' This verse is referring to the striving after the Holy One, blessed be He. So does it not seem that this verse teaches that the striving is free and without effort? We see that it is free, and that is the striving

34. פָּתַח רַבִּי שִׁמְעוֹן בְּרֵישָׁא וְאָמַר, וְיִקְחוּ לִי תְּרוּמָה מֵאֵת כָּל אִישׁ אֲשֶׁר יִדְּבֶנּוּ לִבּוֹ תִּקְחוּ אֶת תְּרוּמָתִי. וְיִקְחוּ לִי, הַאי מַאן דְּבָעֵי לְאִשְׁתַּדְּלָא בְּמִצְוָה. וּלְאִשְׁתַּדְּלָא בֵּיהּ בְּקוּדְשָׁא בְּרִיךְ הוּא, אִצְטְרִיךְ דְּלָא יִשְׁתַּדַּל בֵּיהּ בְּרֵיקַנְיָּא וּבְמַגָּנָא, אֶלָּא אִצְטְרִיךְ לֵיהּ לְבַר נָשׁ לְאִשְׁתַּדְּלָא בֵּיהּ כַּדְקָא יָאוֹת כְּפוּם וְזֵילֵיהּ. וְהָא אוֹקִימְנָא מִלָּה דָּא בְּכַמָּה אַתְרֵי, יָאוֹת לְמֵיסַב בַּר נָשׁ הַהוּא אִשְׁתַּדְּלוּתָא דְּקוּדְשָׁא בְּרִיךְ הוּא. כד"א אִישׁ כְּמַתְּנַת יָדוֹ וְגו'.

35. וְאִי תֵימָא, הָא כְּתִיב לְכוּ שִׁבְרוּ וֶאֱכֹלוּ וּלְכוּ שִׁבְרוּ בְּלֹא כֶסֶף וּבְלֹא מְחִיר יַיִן וְחָלָב, דְּהָא אִיהוּ בְּמַגָּנָא, וְאִיהוּ אִשְׁתַּדְּלוּתָא דְּקוּדְשָׁא בְּרִיךְ הוּא. אֶלָּא אִשְׁתַּדְּלוּתָא דְּאוֹרַיְיתָא, כָּל מַאן דְּבָעֵי זָכֵי בָּהּ. אִשְׁתַּדְּלוּתָא דְּקוּדְשָׁא בְּרִיךְ הוּא לְמִנְדַּע לֵיהּ, כָּל מַאן דְּבָעֵי זָכֵי בֵּיהּ, בְּלֹא אַגְרָא כְּלָל.

after the Holy One, blessed be He." Rav Shimon answers: "Anybody who desires to understand the Torah (spiritual wisdom), merits the wisdom. Anyone who desires to know the Holy One, blessed be He, will merit the knowledge without any payment whatsoever. But if the striving after the Holy One, blessed be He, is in the form of an action, it is prohibited to perform that action halfheartedly and in vain, because one will not merit the drawing down of a spirit of holiness unless he pays in full."

אֲבָל אִשְׁתַּדְלוּתָא דְּקוּדְשָׁא בְּרִיךְ הוּא דְּקַיְּימָא בְּעוֹבָדָא, אָסִיר לְנַטְלָא לֵיהּ לְמַגָּנָא וּבְרֵיקָנְיָיא, בְּגִין דְּלָא זָכֵי בְּהַהוּא עוֹבָדָא כְּלַל, לְאַמְשָׁכָא עֲלֵיהּ רוּחָא דְּקוּדְשָׁא, אֶלָּא בַּאֲגַר שְׁלִים.

In the books of sorcery that Asmodeus, the king of the demons, taught King Solomon: it is written that whoever wants to endeavor to remove from himself the impure spirit and to subdue the spirit of the other side, must pay in full for the action in which he wishes to endeavor, and he should give whatever is requested of him, whether a little or a lot.

36. בְּסִפְרָא דְּחַרְשֵׁי, דְּאוֹלִיף אַשְׁמְדַאי לִשְׁלֹמֹה מַלְכָּא, כָּל מַאן דְּבָעֵי לְאִשְׁתַּדְּלָא לְאַעְבְּרָא מִנֵּיהּ רוּחַ מִסְאָבָא, וּלְאַכְפַּיָיא רוּחָא אָחֳרָא. הַהוּא עוֹבָדָא דְּבָעֵי לְאִשְׁתַּדְּלָא בֵּיהּ, בָּעֵי לְמִקְנֵי לֵיהּ בַּאֲגַר שְׁלִים, בְּכָל מַה דְּיִבְעוֹן מִנֵּיהּ, בֵּין זְעֵיר בֵּין רַב, בְּגִין דְּרוּחַ מִסְאָבָא, אִיהוּ אָזְדַּמַּן תָּדִיר בְּמַגָּנָא וּבְרֵיקָנְיָא,

The spirit of impurity is always ready freely and for nothing, and is available without payment, because the spirit of impurity compels people upon whom he dwells and entices them to dwell with him. He tempts them to make their habitation with him in many ways.

וְאוֹדְבָן בְּלָא אַגְרָא, וְאָנִיס לִבְנֵי נָשָׁא לְמִשְׁרֵי עֲלַיְיהוּ, וּמְפַתֵּי לוֹן לְדַיְירָא עִמְּהוֹן, בְּכַמָּה פִּתּוּיִין, בְּכַמָּה אָרְחִין, סָטֵי לוֹן לְשַׁוָּואָה דִּיּוּרֵיהּ עִמְּהוֹן.

The spirit of holiness is not this way, but only attainable with full payment and great endeavor, and by purifying himself and purifying his habitation with the desire of his heart and soul. And even then, fortunate is he who merits that the spirit of holiness will rest with him. Even with all this, he must be careful to go in the straight path, neither turning right nor left. If he does not, he separates himself immediately and distances himself from the spirit of holiness, and he will not again be able to merit it (his connection) as he did originally.

37. וְרוּחַ קוּדְשָׁא לָאו הָכִי, אֶלָּא בַּאֲגַר שְׁלִים, וּבְאִשְׁתַּדְּלוּתָא רַב סַגִּי, וּבְאִתְדַּכְּאוּתָא דְּגַרְמֵיהּ וּבְאִתְדַּכְּאוּתָא דִּמְשִׁכְנֵיהּ, וּבִרְעוּתָא דְּלִבֵּיהּ וְנַפְשֵׁיהּ. וּכְדֵין זַכָּאָה אִיהוּ דְּיִזְכֵּי לְמִשְׁרֵי בְּמָדוֹרֵיהּ עִמֵּיהּ. וְעִם כָּל דָּא, יִתְהַךְ בְּאֹרַח מֵישָׁר, דְּלָא יִסְטֵי לִימִינָא וְלִשְׂמָאלָא, וְאִי לָאו, בְּיַד אִסְתַּלַּק מִנֵּיהּ, וְאִתְרְחִיק מִנֵּיהּ, וְלָא יָכִיל לְמִשְׁרֵי לֵיהּ כְּדְבְקַדְמֵיתָא.

MEDITATION

Reading this section awakens our understanding and desire to give total commitment and maximum effort to our spiritual work, along with certainty that those actions will bring connection with the Light of the Creator.

וְיִקְחוּ לִי, הַאי מַאן דְּבָעֵי לְאִשְׁתַּדְּלָא
le'ishtadla deba'ei ma'an hai li veyikechu

בְּמִצְוָה, וּלְאִשְׁתַּדְּלָא בֵּיהּ בְּקוּדְשָׁא בְּרִיךְ
berich bekudsha beih ule'ishtadla bemitzvah

הוּא, אִצְטְרִיךְ דְּלָא יִשְׁתַּדַּל בֵּיהּ בְּרֵיקָנְיָיא
bereikanya beih ishtadal dela itzterich hu

וּבְמַגָּנָא, אֶלָּא אִצְטְרִיךְ לֵיהּ לְבַר נָשׁ לְאִשְׁתַּדְּלָא
le'ishtadla nash levar leih itzterich ela uvemagana

בֵּיהּ כַּדְקָא יֵאוֹת כְּפוּם וֵזֵילֵיהּ
cheileih kefum ye'ot kadka beih

'That they should bring Me' means that if someone wishes to undertake a precept—a positive action—and to aspire towards the Holy One, blessed be He, it is necessary that the person not strive halfheartedly and in vain, but rather he should make an effort with all his strength, according to his capacity.

WHEN YOU WANT TO
TURN BACK TIME:

"THIS IS THE BOOK OF THE GENERATIONS OF ADAM"

(ZOHAR, BERESHEET B, VERSE 361)

Sometimes we do things that clearly cause harm to other people, and sometimes it's only later that we realize the harm we have created. Kabbalah provides a means for eliminating the darkness we have brought about; it's a process called *teshuva*. This is often translated as "repentance," but its actual Hebrew root is "return." *Teshuva* is returning to the point before the darkness was created. What's more, through this process of return, we can not only remove the darkness but also change it to Light.

In this section, the Zohar tells of the great gift that was presented to Adam in the form of the Book of Wisdom. The Zohar relates that, when he sinned, Adam acted with the Desire to Receive for the Self Alone and, therefore, he lost the Book of Wisdom. But rather than give up or despair, Adam went through the process of *teshuva* and regained access to the wisdom he had lost. By so doing, Adam opened a channel for all humankind to access the power of *teshuva* and thereby to transform our own negativity into Light.

It is written: "This is the Book of the Generations of Adam," and there literally is a book. We have already explained that when Adam was in the Garden of Eden, God sent a book down to him with Raziel, the holy angel who is in charge of the supernal sacred secrets. In the book were secret inscriptions, and 72 branches of sacred wisdom.

361. זֶה סֵפֶר, סֵפֶר וַדַּאי. וְהָא אוּקִימְנָא, דְּכַד הֲוָה אָדָם בְּגִנְתָא דְּעֵדֶן, נָחִית לֵיהּ קַדִּישָׁא בְּרִיךְ הוּא סִפְרָא, עַל יְדָא דְּרָזִיאֵ"ל, מַלְאָכָא קַדִּישָׁא, מְמַנָּא עַל רָזֵי עִלָּאִין קַדִּישִׁין. וּבֵיהּ גְּלִיפִין, גְּלוּפֵי עִלָּאִין, וְחָכְמָה קַדִּישָׁא, וְשַׁבְעִין וּתְרֵין זִינֵי דְּחָכְמְתָא, הֲווֹ מִתְפָּרְשָׁן מִנֵּיהּ, לְשִׁיתְּ מְאָה וְשַׁבְעִין גְּלִיפִין דְּרָזֵי עִלָּאָה.

In the middle of the book, there is an engraving of Wisdom, which is prepared to receive the 1,500 keys that were not delivered to the supernal Holy Ones. All those secrets were concealed in the book before it came to the hands of Adam. And when he received it, holy angels congregated around him, to hear them and learn them. The angels said, "May God Be exalted, above the heavens. Let your glory be above the earth."

362. בְּאֶמְצָעִיתָא דְּסִפְרָא, גְּלִיפָא דְּחָכְמְתָא, לְמִנְדַּע אֶלֶף וַחֲמֵשׁ מְאָה מַפְתְּחָן, דְּלָא אִתְמְסָרָן לְעִלָּאֵי קַדִּישֵׁי. וְכֻלְּהוּ אַסְתִּימוּ בֵּיהּ בְּסִפְרָא, עַד דְּמָטָא לְגַבֵּי דְּאָדָם, הֲווֹ מִתְכַּנְּשֵׁי מַלְאָכֵי עִלָּאֵי, לְמִנְדַּע וּלְמִשְׁמַע, וַהֲווֹ אָמְרֵי, רוּמָה עַל הַשָּׁמַיִם אֱלֹקִים עַל כָּל הָאָרֶץ כְּבוֹדֶךָ.

The holy angel Hadarniel whispered to Adam and said: "Adam, Adam, conceal the

363. בָּהּ שַׁעֲתָא, אִתְרְמִיז לְגַבֵּיהּ הֲדַרְנִיאֵ"ל מַלְאָכָא קַדִּישָׁא, וַאֲמַר לֵיהּ:

glory of your Master, do not reveal it to the angels, for permission was given to you alone, and not even to the angels, to know the glory of your Master." Therefore, Hadarniel concealed it with Adam until he left the Garden of Eden.

אָדָם אָדָם, הֲוֵי גָּנִיז יְקָרָא דְּמָארָךְ, דְּלָא אִתְיְיהֵיב רְשׁוּתָא לְעֶלָּאֵי, לְמִנְדַּע בִּיקָרָא דְּמָרְךְ, בַּר אַנְתְּ. וַהֲוָה עֲמֵיהּ טָמִיר וְגָנִיז, הַהוּא סִפְרָא, עַד דְּנָפַק אָדָם מִגִּנְתָא דְּעֵדֶן.

In the beginning, Adam studied and used the secrets of his Master every day. Spiritual secrets that none of the angels knew were revealed to him. But when he transgressed the commands of his Master by eating of the Tree of Knowledge, the book flew away from him. Because of this, Adam would strike his head and weep. To repent, he went into the waters of the River Gichon up to his neck, until his body became wrinkled and porous and his radiance changed.

364. דְּהָא בְּקַדְמֵיתָא, הֲוָה מְעַיֵּין בֵּיהּ, וּמִשְׁתַּמֵּשׁ כָּל יוֹמָא בְּגִינְזָא דְּמָרֵיהּ, וְאִתְגַּלְיָין לֵיהּ רָזִין עִלָּאִין, מַה דְּלָא יַדְעוּ שַׁמָּשֵׁי עִלָּאִין. כֵּיוָן דְּחָזְטָא, וְעָבַר עַל פִּקּוּדָא דְּמָארֵיהּ, פָּרְחוּ הַהוּא סִפְרָא מִנֵּיהּ. וַהֲוָה אָדָם טָפַח עַל רֵישׁוֹי, וּבָכֵי, וְעָאל בְּמֵי גִּיחוֹן עַד קְדָלֵיהּ, וּמַיָּיא עָבְדִין גּוּפֵיהּ חֲלָדִין חֲלָדִין, וְאִשְׁתַּנֵּי זִיוֵיהּ.

At that point, God directed the Angel Rafael to return the book to Adam. Adam studied it. He left it to Shet, his son, and to all the generations after him until Abraham. Abraham knew

365. בְּשַׁעֲתָא הַהִיא, רָמַז קֻדְשָׁא בְּרִיךְ הוּא לִרְפָאֵל, וְאָתֵיב לֵיהּ הַהוּא סִפְרָא. וּבֵיהּ הֲוָה מִשְׁתַּדַּל אָדָם, וַאֲנָח לֵיהּ לְשֵׁת בְּרֵיהּ.

how to use the book to examine his Master's Glory. This has already been explained. This book was also given to Chanoch, and through it, Chanoch perceived the Supernal Glory.

וְכֵן לְכָל אִינוּן תּוֹלְדוֹת. עַד דִּמְטָא לְאַבְרָהָם, וּבֵיהּ הֲוָה יָדַע לְאִסְתַּכְּלָא בִּיקָרָא דְּמָארֵיהּ. וְהָא אִתְּמַר. וְכֵן לַחֲנוֹךְ, אִתְיְיהֵב לֵיהּ סִפְרָא, וְאִסְתַּכַּל מִנֵּיהּ, בִּיקָרָא עִלָּאָה.

Meditation

Through this meditation we are connected to Adam's original act of *teshuva*. More important, we can use the channel Adam opened to make spiritual corrections of our own and to transform any darkness we have created into Light.

וַהֲוָה אָדָם טֹפַּח עַל רֵישׁוֹי, וּבְכֵי,
uvachei reisho'i al tofe'ach adam vahavah

וְעָאל בְּמֵי גִּיחוֹן עַד קָדְכֵיה, וּמַיָּא
umaya kadleih ad Gichon bemei ve'al

עָבְדִין גּוּפֵיה חַלְדִין חַלְדִין, וְאִשְׁתַּנֵּי זִיוֵיה.
ziveih ve'shtanei chaladin chaladin gufeih avdin

Because of this, Adam would strike his head and weep. To repent, he went into the waters of the River Gichon up to his neck, until his body became wrinkled and porous and his radiance changed.

110

AWAKENING DESIRE FOR

THE LIGHT:

"HE NEITHER DID EAT BREAD NOR DRINK WATER"

(ZOHAR, SHEMOT, VERSE 251)

Sometimes we encounter challenges, chaos, or simply a feeling of emptiness in our lives. Kabbalah explains that we've been given tools to make those situations better and to bring Light to them. To access these tools, each of us must go through an important process. We must initiate and continuously enlarge our experience of the Light of the Creator. Each of us must strengthen our personal connection with the Light. This growing spiritual experience will become a tremendous source of fulfillment in our lives.

Here the Zohar describes the deep connection with the Light, which Rav Shimon and Rav Elazar experienced through learning the secrets of the Zohar. Their fulfillment was so complete that they felt no physical needs: They "did neither eat bread nor drink water."

Rav Shimon sat while his son, Rav Elazar, stood and explained the secrets of the words of wisdom, and his face shone like the sun. And the words spread and flew in the sky. They sat two days and neither ate nor drank, and they did not know if it was day or night. When they went out, they realized that already two days had passed and they had eaten nothing. Rav Shimon exclaimed: "And he was there with God forty days and forty nights, he did neither eat bread nor drink water." If for us we merited to connect or cleave to God for a while, it was that we spent two days and did not know where we were. For Moses, about whom the Torah bears witness: "And he was there with God forty days" — it is much more so.

251. יָתִיב ר' שִׁמְעוֹן, ור' אֶלְעָזָר בְּרֵיהּ קָאִים וּמְפָרֵשׁ מִלֵּי דְרָזֵי דְחָכְמְתָא, וַהֲווֹ אַנְפּוֹי נְהִירִין כְּשִׁמְשָׁא. וּמִלִּין מִתְפַּשְׁטִין וְטָאסִין בִּרְקִיעָא. יָתְבוּ תְּרֵין יוֹמִין דְּלָא אָכְלוּ וְלָא שָׁתוּ, וְלָא הֲווֹ יַדְעִין אִי הֲוָה יְמָמָא אוֹ לֵילְיָא. כַּד נָפְקוּ, יָדְעוּ דַּהֲווֹ תְּרֵין יוֹמִין דְּלָא טָעֲמוּ מִידֵי. קָרָא עַל דָּא רִבִּי שִׁמְעוֹן, וַיְהִי שָׁם עִם ה' אַרְבָּעִים יוֹם וְאַרְבָּעִים לַיְלָה לֶחֶם לֹא אָכַל וְגו'. וּמָה אִי אֲנָן בְּשַׁעֲתָא חֲדָא כָּךְ, מֹשֶׁה, דִּקְרָא אַסְהִיד בֵּיהּ, וַיְהִי שָׁם עִם ה' אַרְבָּעִים יוֹם וְגו', עַל אַחַת כַּמָּה וְכַמָּה.

When Rav Chiya came before his father, Rav Shimon ben Gamliel, and told of this, Rav Shimon ben Gamliel was amazed and said to him: "My son, Rav Shimon bar Yochai is a lion, and his son Rav Elazar is a lion, and Rav Shimon is not like the other lions.

252. כַּד אָתָא רִבִּי וְחִיָּיא קָמֵיהּ דְּרִבִּי, וְסָח לֵיהּ עוֹבָדָא, תָּוָה רִבִּי, וְאָמַר לֵיהּ ר' שִׁמְעוֹן בֶּן גַּמְלִיאֵל אָבוּי, בְּרִי, ר' שִׁמְעוֹן בֶּן יוֹחַאי אַרְיָא, וְרִבִּי אֶלְעָזָר בְּרֵיהּ אַרְיָא,

"About him it is written: 'A lion has roared, who will not fear?' Now that the higher worlds tremble before him, we certainly tremble. He is a man who never decreed a fast for what he asked or prayed for. He would simply decree, and God would fulfill. God decrees and he annuls. This is what we have learned from the passage: 'He that rules over men must be just, ruling in the fear of God.' God rules over man, and who rules over God, but the righteous man. For God decrees and the righteous man annuls it."

וְלָאו ר' שִׁמְעוֹן כִּשְׁאָר
אַרְיָוָותָא, עֲלֵיהּ כְּתִיב אַרְיֵה
שָׁאָג מִי לֹא יִירָא וְגוֹ'. וּמַה
עָלְמִין דִּלְעֵילָא מִזְדַּעְזְעִין
מִינֵּיהּ, אֲנָן עאכ"ו. גַּבְרָא דְּלָא
גְּזַר תַּעֲנִיתָא לְעָלְמִין עַל מַה
דְּשָׁאִיל וּבָעֵי, אֶלָּא הוּא גּוֹזַר,
קוּדְשָׁא בְּרִיךְ הוּא מְקַיֵּים.
קוּדְשָׁא בְּרִיךְ הוּא גּוֹזַר, וְאִיהוּ
מְבַטֵּל. וְהַיְינוּ דִּתְנָן, מַאי
דִּכְתִיב מוֹשֵׁל בָּאָדָם צַדִּיק
מוֹשֵׁל יִרְאַת אֱלֹהִים, הַקוּדְשָׁא
בְּרִיךְ הוּא מוֹשֵׁל בָּאָדָם, וּמִי
מוֹשֵׁל בְּהַקוּדְשָׁא בְּרִיךְ הוּא,
צַדִּיק. דְּאִיהוּ גּוֹזַר גְּזֵרָה,
וְהַצַּדִּיק מְבַטְּלָהּ.

> ## MEDITATION
>
> With this meditation, we awaken both our desire and our need to experience the Light of the Creator. By meditating on these words, we can taste the fulfillment that comes with that experience and thereby create a greater yearning for connection with the Light.

יָתִיב ר' שִׁמְעוֹן, וְר' אֶלְעָזָר בְּרֵיהּ קָאֵים
ka'eim bereih Elazar veRibbi Shimon Ribbi yativ

וּמְפָרֵשׁ מִלֵּי דְּרָזֵי דְּחָכְמְתָא, וַהֲווֹ אַנְפּוֹי
anpoi vahavo dechachmeta derazei milei umefaresh

נְהִירִין כְּשִׁמְשָׁא. וּמִלִּין מִתְבַּדְּרִין וְטָאסִין
vetasin mitbadrin umilin keshimsha nehirin

בִּרְקִיעָא. יָתְבוּ תְּרֵין יוֹמִין דְּלָא אָכְלוּ
achlu dela yomin terein yatvu birkiya

וְלָא שָׁתוּ, וְלָא הֲווֹ יַדְעִין אִי הֲוָה
havah i yadin havo vela shatu velo

יְמָמָא אוֹ לֵילְיָא.
leilya o yemama

Rav Shimon sat while his son, Rav Elazar, stood and explained the secrets of the words of wisdom, and his face shone like the sun. And the words spread and flew in the sky. They sat two days and neither ate nor drank, and they did not know if it was day or night.

GIVING POWER TO YOUR PRAYERS

(ZOHAR, SHEMOT, VERSE 253)

Have you ever said a prayer with all your heart and soul, and felt that your prayer wasn't answered? To understand what this really means, it's important to see that prayer is not just a way to ask for and receive gifts from on high. Much more important, prayer is a means for gaining closeness and connection with the Creator. This is the real benefit and the true purpose of prayer.

This is made clear in a famous teaching from the Rav of Kotzk. In speaking with his students, the Rav pointed out that, after the sin of Adam, the serpent was cursed to eat dust for all his life. But why was this a punishment, when dust was all the serpent really needed? The Rav of Kotsk explained that this was exactly the point. Since all his needs were met, the serpent would never have reason to truly connect with God. The things we lack in our lives are the very things that awaken our connection with the Creator.

Rav Yehuda said, "There is nothing that is so cherished by God as the prayers of the righteous. Even though it pleases Him, sometimes He grants their request and sometimes He does not."

253. תָּנָן, אָמַר ר' יְהוּדָה, אֵין לָךְ דָּבָר בַּחֲבִיבוּתָא קָמֵי קוּדְשָׁא בְּרִיךְ הוּא, כְּמוֹ תְּפִלָּתָן שֶׁל צַדִּיקִים, וְאַף עַל גַּב דְּנִיחָא לֵיהּ, זִמְנִין דְּעָבֵיד בָּעוּתְהוֹן, וְזִמְנִין דְּלָא עָבֵיד.

Once, the sages have taught, the world needed rain. Rav Eliezer came and decreed forty fasts, but rain did not come. He prayed, but rain did not come. Rav Akiva came, stood and prayed. He said, "He makes the wind to blow," and the wind blew strong and powerful. He said, "And He makes the rain fall" and rain came. Rav Eliezer was crestfallen. Rav Akiva looked into his face saw his discouragement.

254. ת"ר, זִמְנָא חֲדָא הֲוָה עָלְמָא צְרִיכָא לְמִטְרָא, אָתָא רַבִּי אֱלִיעֶזֶר, וְגָזַר אַרְבְּעִין תַּעֲנִיתָא, וְלָא אָתָא מִטְרָא, צַלֵּי צְלוֹתָא, וְלָא אָתָא מִטְרָא. אָתָא רַבִּי עֲקִיבָא, וְקָם וְצַלֵּי, אָמַר מַשִּׁיב הָרוּחַ, וְנָשַׁב זִיקָא, אָמַר וּמוֹרִיד הַגֶּשֶׁם, וְאָתָא מִטְרָא. וַחֲלַשׁ דַּעְתֵּיהּ דְּרַבִּי אֱלִיעֶזֶר, אִסְתַּכַּל רַבִּי עֲקִיבָא בְּאַנְפּוֹי.

Rav Akiva stood before the people and said: "I will give an example to explain this situation. Rav Eliezer is like a cherished friend of the king. When he appears before the king, he is greeted and very pleasantly accepted. The king does not want to grant him his wish quickly, because it is so pleasant to speak with him.

255. קָם רִבִּי עֲקִיבָא קָמֵי עַמָּא וְאָמַר, אֶמְשׁוֹל לָכֶם מָשָׁל, לְמָה הַדָּבָר דּוֹמֶה, רִבִּי אֱלִיעֶזֶר דָּמֵי לִרְחִימָא דְּמַלְכָּא, דִּרְחִים לֵיהּ יַתִּיר, וְכַד עָאל קָמֵי מַלְכָּא, נִיחָא לֵיהּ, וְלָא בָּעֵי לְמַיהַן לֵיהּ בָּעוּתֵיהּ בִּבְהִילוּ, כִּי הֵיכִי דְּלָא לִיתְפְּרַשׁ מִנֵּיהּ,

"But I am like a servant of the king who makes a request of him, and the king does not want him to enter the gates of the palace, and does not want not to speak to him. The king says, 'Grant his request immediately and do not let him enter here.' Rav Eliezer is the friend of the king and I am the servant. The king desires to speak with him constantly and not to be away from him. But as for me, the king does not want me to enter the gates of the palace, therefore he immediately grants my wish." Upon hearing this, Rav Eliezer regained his composure.

דְּנִיחָא לֵיהּ דְּלִישְׁתָּעֵי בַּהֲדֵיהּ.
וַאֲנָא דָּמֵי לְעַבְדָּא דְּמַלְכָּא,
דְּבָעָא בָּעוּתֵיהּ קַמֵּיהּ, וְלָא
בָּעֵי מַלְכָּא דְּלֵיעוֹל לְתַרְעֵי
פַלְטְרִין, וכ"ע דְּלִישְׁתָּעֵי
בַּהֲדֵיהּ, אָמַר מַלְכָּא, הָבוּ
לֵיהּ בָּעוּתֵיהּ בִּבְהִילוּ, וְלָא
לֵיעוֹל הָכָא. כָּךְ רַבִּי אֱלִיעֶזֶר
אִיהוּ רְחִימָא דְּמַלְכָּא, וַאֲנָא
עַבְדָּא, וּבָעֵי מַלְכָּא לְאִשְׁתָּעֵי
בַּהֲדֵיהּ כָּל יוֹמָא, וְלָא יִתְפְּרִישׁ
מִנֵּיהּ. וַאֲנָא, לָא בָּעֵי מַלְכָּא
דְּאִיעוֹל תַּרְעֵי דְּפַלְטְרִין. נָח
דַּעְתֵּיהּ דְּרַבִּי אֱלִיעֶזֶר.

MEDITATION

This meditation awakens our understanding of the true meaning of prayer, which is to connect deeply with the Creator, and it empowers our prayers to make that connection.

רְבִּי אֱלִיעֶזֶר דָּמֵי לִרְחִימָא דְּמַלְכָּא, דְּרָחִים לֵיהּ
leih derachim demalka lirchima damei Eliezer Ribbi

יַתִּיר, וְכַד עָאל קָמֵי מַלְכָּא, נִיחָא לֵיהּ, וְלָא בָּעֵי
ba'ei vela leih nicha malka kamei a'al vechad yatir

לְמֵיתָן לֵיהּ בָּעוּתֵיהּ בִּבְהִילוּ, כִּי הֵיכִי דְּלָא
dela heichi ki bivhilu ba'uteih leih lemaytan

לִיתְפָּרֵשׁ מִנֵּיהּ, דְּנִיחָא לֵיהּ דְּלִישְׁתָּעֵי בַּהֲדֵיהּ
bahadeih delishte'ei leih denicha mineh litperash

Rav Eliezer is like a cherished friend of the king. When he appears before the king, he is greeted and very pleasantly accepted. The king does not want to grant him his wish quickly, because it is so pleasant to speak with him.

AWAKENING YOUR DESIRE TO FULFILL YOUR POTENTIAL:

"WHEN RAV SHIMON WANTED TO DEPART FROM THE WORLD"

(ZOHAR, HAAZINU, VERSE 23)

Sometimes you may find yourself thinking, "I'm really a good person," or even, "I'm a truly spiritual person."

While self-esteem is important, complacency is a huge missed opportunity, and the wrong framework in which to see ourselves and our work. Each of us came to this world with a mission—and our goal is not simply to be "good" or "spiritual" people, but to complete the mission for which we came. If we don't complete our unique mission, the Light we were meant to reveal will remain hidden.

As this section shows, when Rav Shimon chose to leave this world he was determined not to do so in shame, without revealing all the Light and the secrets he was meant to reveal. We should each feel that same commitment and urgency, because it's easy to become complacent in our spiritual work. It's easy to think, "I've done this much, so I'm okay." But this is the wrong standard by which to judge ourselves. Our work is not just to be spiritually observant, but to fulfill our true purpose in the world and our true potential for revealing Light. Our time here is limited, and this is the urgency that Rav Shimon felt so strongly.

Through the Light revealed by Rav Shimon at the time of his passing, we can again recognize our own purpose in the world: connecting to and revealing the Light, and with it peace, joy, fulfillment, and even immortality. We need a sense of urgency to reach that goal. It is the same sense of urgency that Rav Shimon called upon to complete his own work.

Rav Shimon achieved such connection with the Light that he literally gained power over death. When he left this world, it was by his own choice. Before he departed, Rav Shimon knew that he must reveal all the Light he was meant to reveal. Hence, Rav Shimon decided to reveal all the secrets he had not previously disclosed—that is, all the Light that he was meant to bring into this world. This is an important principle for all of us: Our spiritual work should be completed before we depart. And since we don't know when our departure will take place, a sense of urgency should always be with us.

Rav Shimon's passing is truly a seminal moment in the Zohar. All the great souls who have departed the world are present to assist in this great revelation of Light.

We learned that, on the day Rav Shimon wanted to depart from the world and was putting his affairs in order, the friends gathered in the house of Rav Shimon. Rav Elazar, his son, was before him, and Rav Aba and other friends. Rav Shimon lifted up his eyes and saw that the house had become full. Rav Shimon wept and said: "Another time when I was ill, Rav Pinchas ben Yair was before me, and waited for me until I inquired about my place in the Garden of Eden. When I returned, a fire circled me, which never stopped. No one entered my house except by permission. Now I see the fire has stopped, and behold the house is full."

23. תָּאנָא בְּהַהוּא יוֹמָא דר״ש בָּעָא לְאִסְתַּלְּקָא מִן עָלְמָא, וַהֲוָה מְסַדֵּר מִלּוֹי, אִתְכְּנָשׁוּ חַבְרַיָּיא לְבֵי ר״ש, וַהֲווֹ קַמֵּיהּ ר׳ אֶלְעָזָר בְּרֵיהּ, וְר׳ אַבָּא, וּשְׁאָר חַבְרַיָּיא, וַהֲוָה מַלְיָא בֵּיתָא. זָקִיף עֵינוֹי ר״ש, וְחָמָא דְּאִתְמְלֵי בֵּיתָא. בָּכָה ר״ש וְאָמַר, בְּזִמְנָא אַחֲרָא כַּד הֲוֵינָא בְּבֵי מַרְעֵי, הֲוָה רִבִּי פִּנְחָס בֶּן יָאִיר קַמָּאי, וְעַד דְּבָרִירְנָא דּוּכְתַּאי אוֹרִיכוּ לִי עַד הַשְׁתָּא. וְכַד תַּבְנָא, אַסְחַר אֶשָּׁא מִקַּמָּאי, וּמֵעָלְמִין לָא אִתְפָּסַק, וְלָא הֲוָה עָאל בַּר נָשׁ, אֶלָּא בִּרְשׁוּתָא. וְהַשְׁתָּא חֲמֵינָא דְּאִתְפָּסַק, וְהָא אִתְמְלֵי בֵּיתָא.

While they were sitting, Rav Shimon opened his eyes and saw what he saw, and fire encircled the house. Some of the friends departed, and only Rav Elazar, his son, and Rav Aba remained. The rest of the friends stayed outside. Rav Shimon said to Rav Elazar: "Go out and see if Rav Yitzchak is here, because

24. עַד דַּהֲווֹ יַתְבֵי, פָּתַח עֵינוֹי ר״ש, וְחָמָא מַה דְּחָמָא, וְאַסְחַר אֶשָּׁא בְּבֵיתָא, נַפְקוּ כּוּלְּהוּ, וְאִשְׁתָּאֲרוּ רִבִּי אֶלְעָזָר בְּרֵיהּ, וְרִבִּי אַבָּא. וּשְׁאָר חַבְרַיָּיא יָתְבוּ אַבְרָאי. אר״ש לְרִבִּי אֶלְעָזָר בְּרֵיהּ, פּוּק חֲזֵי, אִי הָכָא רִבִּי יִצְחָק, דַּאֲנָא מְעַרְבְנָא לֵיהּ, אֵימָא

I was a guarantor for him. Tell him to settle his affairs and sit by me. Happy is his portion."

Rav Shimon rose and sat down, laughed and rejoiced. He said, "Where are the friends?" Rav Elazar rose and let them in, and they sat before him. Rav Shimon raised his hands, recited a prayer and was glad. He said, "Let the friends that were present at the assembly, the Idra Raba, come here." Rav Elazar, his son, Rav Aba, Rav Yehuda, Rav Yosi and Rav Chiya stayed, while the others departed. In the meanwhile, Rav Yitzchak entered. Rav Shimon said to him, "How deserved is your portion. How much joy should be added to you on this day." Rav Aba sat behind Rav Shimon and Rav Elazar before him.

Rav Shimon said, "Now it is a time of goodwill, and I want to enter without shame into the World to Come. Here are holy matters that I have not revealed until now. Until now they have been hidden in my heart. I wish

לֵיהּ דִּיסַדֵּר מִלּוֹי, וְיֵתִיב לְגַבָּאי, זַכָּאָה חוּלָקֵיהּ.

25. קָם ר'ע', וְיָתִיב, וְחַיֵיךְ, וְחַדֵּי. אֲמַר, אָן אִינּוּן חַבְרַיָּיא. קָם רִבִּי אֶלְעָזָר, וְאָעִיל לוֹן. יָתְבוּ קָמֵיהּ. זָקִיף יְדוֹי ר'ע', וּמְצַלֵּי צְלוֹתָא, וַחֲדֵי וַחֲדֵי, וְאָמַר, אִינּוּן חַבְרַיָּיא דְּאִשְׁתְּכָחוּ בְּבֵי אִדְּרָא, יֵיתְמְנּוּן הָכָא. נַפְקוּ כֻּלְּהוּ, וְאִשְׁתָּאֲרוּ רִבִּי אֶלְעָזָר בְּרֵיהּ, וְרִבִּי אַבָּא, וְרִבִּי יְהוּדָה, וְרִבִּי יוֹסֵי, וְרִבִּי וַיָּיא. אַדְּהָכִי, עָאל רִבִּי יִצְחָק, א'ל ר'ע', כַּמָּה יָאוּת וְחוּלָקָךְ, כַּמָּה וֵידוּ בְּעֵי לְאִתּוֹסְפָא לָךְ בְּהַאי יוֹמָא, יָתִיב רִבִּי אַבָּא בָּתַר כַּתְפוֹי, וְרִבִּי אֶלְעָזָר קָמֵיהּ.

26. אר'ע', הָא הַשְׁתָּא שַׁעֲתָא דִּרְעוּתָא הוּא, וַאֲנָא בָּעֵינָא לְמֵיעַל בְּלָא כִּסּוּפָא לְעָלְמָא דְּאָתֵי. וְהָא מִלִּין קַדִּישִׁין דְּלָא גָּלֵיאן עַד הַשְׁתָּא. בָּעֵינָא לְגַלָּאָה קָמֵי שְׁכִינְתָּא,

to reveal them before the *Shechinah*, so I can enter through them into the Word to Come, so it shall not be said that I have gone from this world in want.

דְּלָא יֵימְרוּן דְּהָא בִּגְרִיעוּתָא אִסְתַּלַּקְנָא מֵעָלְמָא. וְעַד כְּעַן טְמִירִין הֲווֹ בְּלִבָּאי, לְמֵיעַל בְּהוּ לְעָלְמָא דְּאָתֵי.

"This is how I am going to arrange you: Rav Aba shall write. Rav Elazar, my son shall recite orally, and the other friends shall whisper in their hearts." Rav Aba rose behind his back. Rav Elazar was sitting in front of him. Rav Shimon said, "Rise, my son, for another shall sit in this place." Rav Elazar rose.

27. וְכַךְ אִסְדַּרְנָא לְכוּ, רִבִּי אַבָּא יִכְתּוֹב, וְרִבִּי אֶלְעָזָר בְּרִי יִלְעֵי, וּשְׁאָר חַבְרַיָּיא יְרַחֲשׁוּן בְּלִבַּיְיהוּ. קָם רִבִּי אַבָּא מִבָּתַר כַּתְפוֹי. וְיָתִיב רִבִּי אֶלְעָזָר בְּרֵיהּ קַמֵּיהּ, א׳׳ל קוּם בְּרִי, דְּהָא אַחֲרָא יְתִיב בְּהַהוּא אַתַר, קָם רִבִּי אֶלְעָזָר.

MEDITATION

This meditation has the power to keep you consistently motivated and focused toward achieving your potential. Use it to ignite a feeling of urgency in your spiritual purpose, especially at moments when you begin to feel comfortable or complacent.

אר'ע',   הָא הַשְׁתָּא   שַׁעְתָּא דִּרְעוּתָא הוּא,
hu   diruta   sha'ata   hashta   ha amar Ribbi Shimon

וַאֲנָא בָּעֵינָא לְמֵיעַל בְּלָא כְּסוּפָא לְעָלְמָא דְּאָתֵי.
de'atei le'alma kisufa belo lemei'al ba'eina va'ana

Rav Shimon said, "Now it is a time of goodwill, and I want to enter without shame into the World to Come.

When There's Too Much to Do and You're Feeling Overwhelmed:

"The importance of small openings"

(Zohar, Emor, verse 128)

Sometimes life seems overwhelming, both your everyday life and what's taking place in the world as a whole. There's just too much to do and it's all so hard. That's not a pleasant feeling, but when it comes over you, be aware that the feeling contains some important messages.

First, know that there really *is* too much to do, and there really *are* times when you're "in over your head." But we did not come to this world just to stay within our capabilities. Our purpose in life is to go beyond our capabilities, and to fulfill that purpose we need to connect with the Creator's Light.

That's the hidden message when you feel like life *is* too much for you. You can't handle it by yourself—but you don't have to handle it by yourself. All you have to do is make a small opening by taking a positive action.

Once a student of the great Kabbalist Rav Yehuda Ashlag cried out to his master in despair: "I've done everything I possibly can in my spiritual work, and I still haven't been able to complete it." To the student's surprise, Rav Ashlag seemed quite pleased. "If you've really tried as hard as you can, you've learned that you can't do it by yourself. Now you can ask the Creator for help with all your heart and all your soul."

Connecting with the Light doesn't mean that you have to be a great sage. Just take the first small step. Just make a start, and the Creator will do the rest. Create an opening like "the eye of a needle," and infinite Light will flow through that opening.

Rav Chiya began, "'I sleep, but my heart is awake. My beloved is knocking...' This is the Assembly of Israel saying: 'I sleep in exile in Egypt.' My children were there, in harsh slavery, 'but my heart wakes' to protect them so they will not be destroyed in exile. 'My beloved is knocking,' refers to the Creator, who said: 'And I have remembered My covenant.'

128. וּבַחֹדֶשׁ הָרִאשׁוֹן בְּאַרְבָּעָה עָשָׂר יוֹם לַחֹדֶשׁ וְגוֹ'. רַבִּי חִיָּיא פָּתַח, אֲנִי יְשֵׁנָה וְלִבִּי עֵר קוֹל דּוֹדִי דוֹפֵק וְגוֹ'. אֲמְרָה כְּנֶסֶת יִשְׂרָאֵל, אֲנִי יְשֵׁנָה בְּגָלוּתָא דְמִצְרַיִם, דַּהֲווֹ בָּנַי בְּשִׁעְבּוּדָא דְקַשְׁיוֹ. וְלִבִּי עֵר, לְנַטְרָא לְהוּ דְּלָא יִשְׁתֵּיצוּן בְּגָלוּתָא. קוֹל דּוֹדִי דוֹפֵק, דָּא קוּדְשָׁא בְּרִיךְ הוּא, דְּאָמַר וָאֶזְכּוֹר אֶת בְּרִיתִי.

"'Open to me' means provide for me an opening the size of the eye of a needle, and I shall open to you the celestial gates."

129. פִּתְחִי לִי פִּתְחָא כְּחוּדָא דְמַחֲטָא, וַאֲנָא אַפְתַּח לָךְ תַּרְעִין עִלָּאִין.

MEDITATION

This meditation awakens our awareness that all we need to do is make small openings for the Light of the Creator. It also strengthens the power of the actions that are the openings themselves, to allow the Light to flow through them.

פִּתְחוּ לִי פִּתְחָא כְּחִדּוּדָא דְּמַחֲטָא,
demachata kechiduda pitcha li pitchi

וַאֲנָא אַפְתַּח לְךָ תַּרְעִין עִלָּאִין.
ila'in tarin lecha aftach va'ana

'Open to me' means provide for me an opening the size of the eye of a needle, and I shall open to you the celestial gates.

Erasing the Ego:

"He who is small is great"

(Zohar, Chayei Sarah, verse 21)

When things are going well for you, you should definitely give yourself the credit you deserve—but you may also notice a growing sense of your own importance, which is something you ought to resist. In a similar way, you can feel wounded and angry when something goes wrong in your life. You may want to blame others or to blame yourself. As you become aware of these feelings, keep an important principle of Kabbalah in mind: To the degree that your ego is smaller, your connection with the Light grows stronger; to the degree that your ego enlarges, your connection weakens. It's an ongoing and exact balance.

The Zohar explains that both inflated self-importance and excessive self-deprecation are signs that your ego is taking control. Unlike the soul—whose only desires to connect with the Light of the Creator—the ego always has an agenda. It's the ego's nature to be angry when its agenda isn't being met, and also to be complacent and self-satisfied when the agenda seems to be fulfilled. These feelings are two sides of the same coin, and both can block connection with the Light.

When the Zohar speaks of "the small being great," this refers to the absence of ego in a truly righteous person. In this section below, this point is made through the kabbalistic meaning of Sarah's age. Sarah died when she was 127 years old. In relating this number, the Torah expresses it as three parts: one hundred year (in the singular), twenty year (again singular), and then seven years (in the plural). This indicates that the smallest of the numbers has the greatest significance. The secret of this: *less* ego makes a person *more*—that is, more connected to the Creator's Light.

Happy is he who makes less of himself in this world, for how great and high he is in the Eternal World. The head of the Supernal Academy spoke to that effect, saying that whoever is small is great. He who is great in this world is small in the Eternal World, as it is written: "'And Sarah's life was a hundred year...' A hundred, which is a large number, is followed by the word 'year,' in the singular. Yet seven, which is a small number, was greatly increased, for it is followed by the plural word 'years.' Come and behold: The Creator only makes greater the person who lessens himself. He diminishes only the person who makes himself great. Happy is he who diminishes himself in this world. How great he is above in the Eternal World."

21. זַכָּאָה אִיהוּ, מַאן דְּאַזְעֵיר גַּרְמֵיהּ, בְּהַאי עַלְמָא, כַּמָּה אִיהוּ רַב וְעִלָּאָה, בְּהַהוּא עַלְמָא. וְהָכִי פָּתַח רַב מְתִיבְתָּא, מַאן דְּאִיהוּ זְעֵיר, אִיהוּ רַב. מַאן דְּאִיהוּ רַב, אִיהוּ זְעֵיר. דִּכְתִיב וַיִּהְיוּ חַיֵּי שָׂרָה וְגו'. מֵאָה, דְּאִיהוּ חוּשְׁבַּן רַב, כְּתִיב בֵּיהּ שָׁנָה, וְזַעֵירוּ דִשְׁנִין, חַד, אַזְעֵיר לֵיהּ. שֶׁבַע דְּאִיהוּ חוּשְׁבַּן זְעֵיר, אַסְגֵּי לֵיהּ וְרַבֵּי לֵיהּ, דִּכְתִיב שָׁנִים. תָּא חֲזֵי, דְּלָא רַבֵּי קוּדְשָׁא בְּרִיךְ הוּא, אֶלָּא לִדְאַזְעֵיר, וְלָא אַזְעֵיר, אֶלָּא לִדְרַבֵּי, זַכָּאָה אִיהוּ, מַאן דְּאַזְעֵיר גַּרְמֵיהּ בְּהַאי עַלְמָא, כַּמָּה אִיהוּ רַב בְּעִלּוּיָא. לְהַהוּא עַלְמָא (עַד כָּאן).

MEDITATION

This meditation diminishes your ego. When you sense
that your ego is getting the best of you, use this meditation to reduce your ego's influence and thereby
strengthen your connection to the Light.

זַכָּאָה אִיהוּ, מַאן דְּאַזְעִיר גַּרְמֵיהּ, בְּהַאי עַלְמָא,

alma beha'i garmeih de'azeir ma'an ihu zaka'ah

כַּמָה אִיהוּ רַב וְעִלָּאָה, בְּהַהוּא עַלְמָא.

alma behahu ve'ila'ah rav ihu kamah

*Happy is he who diminishes himself in this world. How
great he is above in the Eternal World.*

Having Certainty in the Spiritual System, Even When the Outcome Is in Doubt

(Zohar, Mishpatim, verse 99)

As you move forward in your spiritual work, you have the expectation that the work will influence physical and material outcomes in all areas of your life. But there may be times when you feel that the Light is not being revealed in the way you expected. You may lose a major deal, for example, or an important personal relationship may deteriorate. When such things happen, people sometimes stop there—not because they feel they've achieved their goal, but because they become disheartened that they ever will.

Revelation of the Creator's Light does not come when or how we expect it—but it *will* come. The Light reveals itself in glimpses, in different ways and at different times. We merit these glimpses by constantly and consistently yearning and seeking them. That's what this reading is really about. As we move forward in our spiritual study, those glimpses of Light will expand into a deeper and longer connection.

In this section of the Zohar, a wise teacher explains that the Torah discloses its spiritual wisdom little by little—like a lover peeking out of a hiding place for only a moment before quickly disappearing again. We live in a world of concealment. In this dimension of reality, the Light of the Creator is not revealed everywhere, or all the time. Connection with the Light, therefore, is an ongoing process of disclosure and concealment. This process is not governed by our expectations, especially if we expect revelation to happen right away. But when the Light does reveal itself, our continuous yearning allows us to grasp that Light. Through this process, we can continually grow our connection to the Light and the manifestation of it in our life. The Zohar makes very clear that only those who are constantly searching for the Creator's Light will merit finding and growing it.

The portion of the Torah referred to in this passage does not refer only to biblical stories or information. In a larger sense, Torah is the essence of the Creator. Here the Zohar speaks about the relationship between that essence and those who seek it.

This is likened to a beautiful and beloved woman who hides in her chamber. She has a secret lover. Her lover, because of the love he feels for her, passes around the gate of her house and looks for her. She knows that her lover always goes around her house's gate, so she opens a small window in her hidden chamber, and reveals her face to her lover for just an instant. Then immediately she is concealed again. None of those who were with her lover saw this — only her lover, whose body, mind, and soul go out to her. And he knows that because of the love she has for him, she is revealed to him for a moment to arouse the love. It is so also with the spiritual wisdom that is revealed only to its lover. The Torah knows that the wise of heart pace around its gate every day, so it reveals its face to him from within the chamber and then immediately returns to its place to be hidden again. None of those who were with him knew or beheld the Torah, but only he himself goes to the Torah, in body,

99. מְתַל לְמַה'ד, לִרְחִימָתָא,
דְּאִיהִי שַׁפִּירְתָא בְּחֵיזוּ,
וּשַׁפִּירְתָא בְּרֵיוָא, וְאִיהִי
טְמִירְתָא בִּטְמִירוּ גּוֹ הֵיכְלָא
דִּילָהּ, וְאִית לָהּ רְחִימָא
יְחִידָאָה, דְּלָא יַדְעִין בֵּיהּ בְּנֵי
נָשָׁא, אֶלָּא אִיהוּ בִּטְמִירוּ.
הַהוּא רְחִימָא, מִגּוֹ רְחִימָא
דִּרְחִים לָהּ עָבַר לְתַרְעָא בֵּיתָהּ
תָּדִיר, זָקִיף עֵינוֹי לְכָל סְטָר.
אִיהִי, יַדְעַת דְּהָא רְחִימָא
אַסְחַר תַּרְעָא בֵּיתָהּ תָּדִיר, מָה
עָבְדַת, פָּתְחַת פִּתְחָא זְעֵירָא
בְּהַהוּא הֵיכְלָא טְמִירָא, דְּאִיהִי
תַּמָּן, וּגְלִיאַת אַנְפָּהָא לְגַבֵּי
רְחִימָאָה, וּמִיָּד אִתְהַדְּרַת
וְאִתְכַּסִּיאַת. כָּל אִינּוּן דְּהֲווֹ
לְגַבֵּי רְחִימָא, לָא חֲמוּ וְלָא
אִסְתַּכְּלוּ, בַּר רְחִימָא בִּלְחוֹדוֹי,
וּמְעוֹי וְלִבֵּיהּ וְנַפְשֵׁיהּ אֲזָלוּ
אֲבַתְרָהּ. וְיָדַע דְּמִגּוֹ רְחִימוּ
דִּרְחִימַת לֵיהּ, אִתְגַּלְיַאת לְגַבֵּיהּ
רִגְעָא חֲדָא, לְאִתְעָרָא רְחִימוּ
לֵיהּ. הָכִי הוּא מִלָּה דְּאוֹרַיְיתָא,
לָא אִתְגַּלְיַאת, אֶלָּא לְגַבֵּי
רְחִימָאָה. יַדְעַת אוֹרַיְיתָא,
דְּהַהוּא חַכִּימָא דְּלִבָּא אַסְחַר
לְתַרְעָא בֵּיתָהּ כָּל יוֹמָא, מָה
עָבְדַת, גְּלִיאַת אַנְפָּהָא לְגַבֵּיהּ,

and soul. Hence the Torah is both revealed and concealed, and lovingly goes to its lover to arouse his love.

מִגּוֹ הֵיכְלָא, וְאַרְמִיזַת לֵיהּ
רְמִיזָא, וּמִיָּד אַהֲדְרַת לְאַתְרָהּ
וְאִתְטַמְּרַת. כָּל אִנּוּן דְּתַמָּן,
לָא יַדְעֵי, וְלָא מִסְתַּכְּלֵי, אֶלָּא
אִיהוּ בִּלְחוֹדוֹי, וּמֵעוֹי וְלִבֵּיהּ
וְנַפְשֵׁיהּ אָזִיל אֲבַתְרָהּ. וְעַ"ד,
אוֹרַיְיתָא אִתְגַּלְיָאת וְאִתְכַּסְיָאת,
וְאָזְלַת בִּרְחִימוּ לְגַבֵּי רְחִימָהָא,
לְאִתְעָרָא בַּהֲדֵיהּ רְחִימוּ.

Come and see: such is the way of the Torah. At first, when it begins to be revealed to man, it gives him a slight hint. If he recognizes it, very well — but if he does not, it sends for him and calls him a fool. The Torah says to whoever it sends for: "Tell that fool to come here so I can talk to him." This is the meaning of, "Whoever is simple, let him turn in here: and as for him that lacks understanding..." When that foolish person approaches, the Torah begins by speaking to him from behind the veil that it spreads before him. It speaks to him according to his understanding, until little by little he will pay attention. This level of homiletic interpretation is known as *Drash*.

100. ת"ח, אָרְחָא דְּאוֹרַיְיתָא
כָּךְ הוּא, בְּקַדְמֵיתָא כַּד שַׁרְיָא
לְאִתְגַּלְּאָה לְגַבֵּי בַּר נָשׁ,
אַרְמִיזַת לֵיהּ בִּרְמִיזוּ, אִי יָדַע
טָב. וְאִי לָא יָדַע, שַׁדְּרַת
לְגַבֵּיהּ, וְקָרְאַת לֵיהּ פֶּתִי.
וְאָמְרַת אוֹרַיְיתָא, לְהַהוּא
דְּשַׁדְּרַת לְגַבֵּיהּ, אִמְרוּ לְהַהוּא
פֶּתִי, דְּיִקְרַב הָכָא, וְאִשְׁתָּעֵי
בַּהֲדֵיהּ. הֲדָא הוּא דִּכְתִיב, מִי פֶתִי יָסֻר
הֵנָּה וְחֲסַר לֵב וְגוֹ'. קָרִיב
לְגַבָּהּ, שָׁרִיאַת לְמַלְּלָא עִמֵּיהּ,
מִבָּתַר פָּרוֹכְתָּא דְּפַרְסָא לֵיהּ,
מִלִּין לְפוּם אָרְחוֹי, עַד
דְּיִסְתַּכַּל זְעֵיר זְעֵיר, וְדָא הוּא
דְּרָשָׁא.

101. Later it speaks with him in riddles from behind a thin sheet. This is the level known as *Haggadah*. If he frequently returns, the Torah is revealed to him face to face, and tells him all the obscure secrets and obscure ways that were hidden in its heart since the ancient days. Then that man is a ruler, a man of the Torah, the master of the house, because the Torah revealed to him all its secrets and has not kept or concealed anything from him.

101. לְבָתַר, תִּשְׁתָּעֵי בַּהֲדֵיהּ, מִבָּתַר שׁוּשִׁיפָא דָקִיק, מִלִּין דִּוְחִידָה, וְדָא אִיהוּ הַגָּדָה. לְבָתַר דְּאִיהוּ רָגִיל לְגַבָּהּ, אִתְגַּלְיַאת לְגַבֵּיהּ אַנְפִּין בְּאַנְפִּין, וּמְלִילַת בַּהֲדֵיהּ כָּל רָזִין סְתִימִין דִּילָהּ, וְכָל אָרְחִין סְתִימִין, דַּהֲווֹ בְּלִבְּאָה טְמִירִין, מִיּוֹמִין קַדְמָאִין. כְּדֵין אִיהוּ בַּר נָשׁ שְׁלִים, בַּעַל תּוֹרָה וַדַּאי, מָארֵי דְּבֵיתָא, דְּהָא כָּל רָזִין דִּילָהּ גְּלִיאַת לֵיהּ, וְלָא רְוִוחָקַת, וְלָא כַּסִּיאַת מִינֵּיהּ כְּלוּם.

102. The Torah said to him: "Recall the allusion I gave you in the beginning. These are the secrets that were contained in that allusion." He then sees that one must not add to or diminish the words of the Torah. The literal meaning is as it is, so that not even one letter should be added or taken away. Therefore the people of the world must take heed to pursue the Torah and love it, as we learned.

102. אָמְרָה לֵיהּ, וְחָמֵית מִלָּה דִּרְמִיזָא דְּקָא רָמִיזְנָא לָךְ בְּקַדְמֵיתָא, כָּךְ וְכָךְ רָזִין הֲווֹ, כָּךְ וְכָךְ הוּא. כְּדֵין חָמֵי, דְּעַל אִינּוּן מִלִּין לָאו לְאוֹסָפָא, וְלָאו לְמִגְרַע מִנַּיְיהוּ. וּכְדֵין פְּשָׁטֵיהּ דִּקְרָא, כְּמָה דְּאִיהוּ, דְּלָאו לְאוֹסָפָא וְלָא לְמִגְרַע אֲפִילוּ אָת חַד. וְעַל דָּא, בְּנֵי נָשָׁא אִצְטְרִיכוּ לְאִזְדַּהֲרָא, לְמִרְדַּף אֲבַתְרָא דְּאוֹרַיְיתָא, לְמֶהֱוֵי רְחִימִין דִּילָהּ, כְּמָה דְּאִתְּמַר.

MEDITATION

This meditation awakens our understanding of the workings of the spiritual system. It helps us not to be discouraged when the Light is not revealed when and how we want it. It gives us the power to constantly yearn and search for revelations—and grab for them when they occur.

לְבָתַר דְּאִיהוּ רָגִיל לְגַבָּה, אִתְגְּלִיאַת לְגַבֵּיהּ
legabeih itgeli'at legavah ragil de'ihu levatar

אַנְפִּין בְּאַנְפִּין, וּמְלִילַת בַּהֲדֵיהּ כָּל רָזִין סְתִימִין
stimin razin kol bahadeih umelilat be'anpin anpin

דִּילָהּ, וְכָל אָרְחִין סְתִימִין, דַּהֲווֹ בְּלִבָּאהּ
belibah dahavo stimin archin vechol dilah

טְמִירִין, מִיּוֹמִין קַדְמָאִין.
kadma'in miyomin temirin

If he frequently returns, the Torah is revealed to him face to face, and tells him all the obscure secrets and obscure ways that were hidden in its heart since ancient days.

PREPARATION

(ZOHAR, NOACH, VERSE 273)

Like any important endeavor, studying the Zohar and other spiritual work should be done with preparation, focused attention, and respect. The purpose of respect is not simply to show honor. Respect is a physical manifestation of our consciousness—and our consciousness is the Vessel in which Light can manifest.

Neither study nor action can create deep connection with the Light if they're done in a haphazard way. In fact, the opposite is true: The amount of Light revealed by your study and action will be in direct proportion to the preparation you've done.

In this section, Rav Yehuda awakens in the middle of the night and begins speaking about spiritual matters. Another traveler, who is also awake, begins to ask him questions. But Rav Yehuda tells the traveler that he can't discuss spiritual matters while simply lying in bed. Such a discussion requires careful preparation in mind, heart, and soul. Preparation expresses respect for both the act of studying and the Light it reveals. The greater our consciousness of respect, the stronger our connection will be.

Rav Yehuda awoke one night to study. It was midnight, in a guest house in the town of Mata-Machesya. There was another traveler staying there, who had arrived with two sacks of clothes to sell. Rav Yehuda opened the discussion, saying, "And this stone which I have set for a pillar shall be the house of God." He continued, "That stone is the Foundation Stone, on which the world was established. And on that stone the Holy Temple was built!"

The other traveler raised his head and said: "How can this be possible? For the Foundation Stone existed before the world was created: and from it the world was established. You claim that: 'this stone which I have set for a pillar' means that until Yaakov set it as a pillar, it was not properly in its place. As it is written: 'And he took the stone he had put under his head.' But the Foundation Stone was established and stood in its place before the creation of the world. And furthermore,

273. רַבִּי יְהוּדָה, קָם לֵילְיָא
וַד לְמִלְעֵי בְּאוֹרַיְיתָא, בְּפַלְגּוּ
לֵילְיָא, בְּבֵי אוּשְׁפִּיזָא, בְּמָתָא
מְחַסְיָא. וַהֲוָה תַּמָּן בְּבֵיתָא, וַד
יוּדָאי, דְּאָתָא בָּתְרֵי קְסִירָא
דִּקְטִפִּירָא. פָּתַח רַבִּי יְהוּדָה
וַאֲמַר, וְהָאֶבֶן הַזֹּאת אֲשֶׁר
שַׂמְתִּי מַצֵּבָה יִהְיֶה בֵּית
אֱלֹקִים. דָּא הִיא אֶבֶן שְׁתִיָּה,
דְּמִתַּמָּן אִשְׁתִּיל עָלְמָא, וַעֲלָהּ
אִתְבְּנֵי בֵּי מַקְדְּשָׁא.

274. זָקַף רֵישֵׁיהּ, הַהוּא יוּדָאי
וְאָמַר לוֹ הַאי מִלָּה אֵיךְ
אֶפְשָׁר, וְהָא אֶבֶן שְׁתִיָּה עַד
לָא אִתְבְּרֵי עָלְמָא הֲוַת, וּמִינָהּ
אִשְׁתִּיל עָלְמָא, וְאַתְּ אֲמַרְתְּ
וְהָאֶבֶן הַזֹּאת אֲשֶׁר שַׂמְתִּי
מַצֵּבָה. דְּמַשְׁמַע דְּיַעֲקֹב שַׁוֵּי
לָהּ הַשְׁתָּא, דִּכְתִיב וַיִּקַּח אֶת
הָאֶבֶן אֲשֶׁר שָׂם מְרַאֲשֹׁתָיו.
וְתוּ, דְּיַעֲקֹב בְּבֵית אֵל הֲוָה,
וְהַאי אַבְנָא הֲוָה בִּירוּשָׁלֵם.

Yaakov was in Bet-El, while the Foundation Stone was in Jerusalem, where it stands in the place of the Holy Temple."

Rav Yehuda, without turning his face toward him, quoted the verse, "'Prepare to meet your God, O Israel.' He continued, as it is written: 'Take heed and hear, O Israel.' This means that the words of Torah (spiritual wisdom) require full attention. It should never be approached without the body and soul properly focused." The other traveler rose, dressed, sat by Rav Yehuda's side, and said: "Happy are you righteous who study the Torah day and night!"

Rav Yehuda said to him: "Now that you have properly prepared yourself, we shall converse with one another, and you can say what you want to say. For before discussing Torah a person should properly prepare his body and heart. If this were not so, I would lie in bed and think of these things in my heart. But we have learned

275. רַבִּי יְהוּדָה, לָא אַסְחַר רֵישֵׁיהּ לְגַבֵּיהּ, פְּתַח וַאֲמַר הִכּוֹן לִקְרַאת אֱלֹהֶיךָ יִשְׂרָאֵל. וּכְתִיב הַסְכֵּת וּשְׁמַע יִשְׂרָאֵל. מִלֵּי דְאוֹרַיְיתָא בָּעְיָין כַּוָּנָה. וּמִלִּין דְּאוֹרַיְיתָא, בָּעָאן לְאִתְתַּקְנָא בְּגוּפָא וּרְעוּתָא כַּחֲדָא. קָם הַהוּא יוּדָאי, וְאִתְלַבַּשׁ, וְיָתִיב לְגַבֵּיהּ דְּרַבִּי יְהוּדָה, וַאֲמַר זַכָּאִין אַתּוּן צַדִּיקַיָּא, דְּמִשְׁתַּדְלֵי בְּאוֹרַיְיתָא יוֹמָא וְלֵילֵי.

276. אָמַר לוֹ רַבִּי יְהוּדָה, הַשְׁתָּא דְּכַוְּונַת גַּרְמָךְ, אֵימָא מִילָךְ, דְּנִתְחַבֵּר כַּחֲדָא. דְּהָא מִלֵּי דְאוֹרַיְיתָא בָּעְיָין תִּקּוּנָא דְּגוּפָא, וְתִקּוּנָא דְלִבָּא. וְאִי לָאו, בְּעַרְסָאי שְׁכִיבְנָא וּבְלִבָּאי אֲמַרְנָא מִלִּין. אֶלָּא הָא תָּנִינָן, דַּאֲפִילוּ חַד דְּיָתִיב וְלָעֵי בְּאוֹרַיְיתָא שְׁכִינְתָּא

that even one person sitting and studying Torah is accompanied by the *Shechinah*. And if the *Shechinah* is already here, how can I lay in bed? Also, in order to delve into Torah, a person needs a clear mind, and he who lies in bed does not have a clear mind.

"Furthermore, when a person awakens to study Torah in the middle of the night, when the northern wind awakes, the Creator enters the Garden of Eden and enjoys the company of the righteous. And He, together with the righteous in the Garden, listen to the words that come from that person's mouth. So if the Creator and the righteous delight in hearing the words of Torah at this hour, how can I lie in my bed?" "So now," Rav Yehuda told the traveler, "Say what you have to say."

אִתְוַוזְּבְרַת בַּהֲדֵיהּ, וּמַה שְׁכִינְתָּא הָכָא, וַאֲנָא שָׁכִיב בְּעַרְסַאי. וְלָא עוֹד, אֶלָּא דְּבָעֵיין צְחוּתָא.

277. וְתוּ, דְּכָל בַּר נָשׁ, דְּקָם לְמִלְעֵי בְּאוֹרַיְיתָא, מִפַּלְגּוּ לֵילְיָא, כַּד אִתְעַר רוּחַ צָפוֹן, קֻדְשָׁא בְּרִיךְ הוּא אָתֵי לְאִשְׁתַּעְשְׁעָא עִם צַדִּיקַיָּא בְּגִנְתָּא דְעֵדֶן. וְהוּא וְכָל צַדִּיקַיָּא דִּבְגִנְתָּא, כֻּלְּהוּ צַיְיתִין לְאַלֵּין מִלִּין דְּנָפְקֵי מִפּוּמֵיהּ. וּמַה קֻדְשָׁא בְּרִיךְ הוּא, וְכָל צַדִּיקַיָּא, מִתְעַדְּנִין לְמִשְׁמַע מִלֵּי דְאוֹרַיְיתָא בְּשַׁעֲתָא דָא. וַאֲנָא אֱהֵא שָׁכִיב בְּעַרְסַאי. אָמַר לֵיהּ, הַשְׁתָּא אֵימָא מִילָךְ.

MEDITATION

This meditation brings understanding of the need to prepare ourselves for spiritual work with the right consciousness. This meditation itself can also be one of the steps in that preparation.

וּכְתִיב הַסְכֵּת וּשְׁמַע יִשְׂרָאֵל. מִלֵּי דְּאוֹרַיְיתָא בָּעְיָין
ba'iyan de'orayita milei Israel ushma hasket uchtiv

כַּוָּנָה. וּמִלִּין דְּאוֹרַיְיתָא, בָּעָאן לְאִתְתַּקָּנָא בְּגוּפָא
begufa le'it'takana ba'an de'orayita umilin kavanah

וּרְעוּתָא כַּחֲדָא.
kachada uruta

'Take heed and hear, O Israel.' This means that the words of Torah (spiritual wisdom) require full attention. It should never be approached without the body and soul properly focused.

III

MEDITATIONS
FOR GREATER
AWARENESS

EXPANDING YOUR YEARNING FOR THE LIGHT:

"THE VISION OF RAV CHIYA"

(ZOHAR, PROLOGUE, VERSE 49)

Sometimes we feel as if something has knocked us off our feet. We feel alone in the dark, with an unshakeable sense of emptiness. At that point, we need to understand that we cannot make it through without the Light of the Creator—and that understanding in itself brings about a yearning for connection. The problems of our everyday lives are there for a reason. We need to face challenges, and even to feel pain, to yearn genuinely for the Light. But once connection with the Light of the Creator has truly become our heartfelt desire, the pain of everyday life in the world vanishes in an almost miraculous way.

In this section, we are taught that Rav Chiya fasted to attain a spiritual level in which he merited his deepest desire—a vision of Rav Shimon and his son, Rav Elazar. His desire for this was so great that he was completely oblivious to the physical pain caused by fasting. When the vision of Rav Shimon was at last finally granted to him, Rav Chiya himself was elevated to a greater connection with the Light of the Creator.

Rav Chiya prostrated himself on the earth. He kissed the dust and cried out: "Dust, dust, how stubborn you are! How shameless you are, that all the delights of the eye perish within you! You consume all the beacons of Light in the world, whom are the righteous people, and grind them into nothing. How impertinent you are! The Sacred Light that illuminated the world, the great leader who governs the entire world and whose merit sustains the world, is consumed by you! Rav Shimon, the Light of the Illumination, the Light of the Worlds, you perish in the dust even while you sustain and govern the world!" Rav Chiya then fell into a reverie for a moment, and then said: "Dust, dust, be not proud! The pillars of the world will not be delivered into your hands! Rav Shimon shall not be consumed by you!"

Weeping, Rav Chiya walked along in the company of Rav Yosi. For forty days he fasted so that he might meet with Rav Shimon. When he was

49. אִשְׁתַּטָּח רַבִּי חִיָּיא בְּאַרְעָא וְנָשִׁיק לְעַפְרָא, וּבָכָה וַאֲמַר, עַפְרָא עַפְרָא, כַּמָּה אַתְּ קְשֵׁי קְדָל, כַּמָּה אַתְּ בְּחוֹצְפָּא, דְּכָל מַחֲמַדֵּי עֵינָא יִתְבְּלוּן בָּךְ, כָּל עַמּוּדֵי נְהוֹרִין דְּעָלְמָא תֵּיכוֹל וְתֵידוּק. כַּמָּה אַתְּ וַוְצִיפָא, בּוֹצִינָא קַדִּישָׁא דַּהֲוָה נָהִיר עָלְמָא שַׁלִּיטָא רַבְרְבָא מְמַנָּא דִּזְכוּתֵיהּ מְקַיֵּים עָלְמָא, אִתְבְּלֵי בָּךְ. רַבִּי שִׁמְעוֹן נְהִירוּ דְּבוֹצִינָא, נְהִירוּ דְּעָלְמִין, אַנְתְּ בְּלֵי בְּעַפְרָא וְאַנְתְּ קַיָּים וְנָהֵג עָלְמָא. אִשְׁתּוֹמֵם רִגְעָא וְזָדָא, וַאֲמַר עַפְרָא עַפְרָא לָא תִתְגָּאֵי, דְּלָא יִתְמַסְרוּן בָּךְ עַמּוּדִין דְּעָלְמָא, דְּהָא רַבִּי שִׁמְעוֹן לָא אִתְבְּלֵי בָּךְ.

50. קָם רַבִּי חִיָּיא וַהֲוָה בָּכֵי. אֲזַל, וְרַבִּי יוֹסֵי עִמֵּיהּ. מֵהַהוּא יוֹמָא אִתְעַנִּי אַרְבְּעִין יוֹמִין לְמֶחֱמֵי לְרַבִּי שִׁמְעוֹן.

148

told, "You are not fit to see him," he wept and fasted for another forty days. Then, in a vision he was shown Rav Shimon and Rav Elazar, his son. They were discussing the interpretation of that certain world which Rav Yosi had mentioned in the name of Rav Shimon. And many thousands were listening to their words.

אָמְרוּ לֵיהּ לֵית אַנְתְּ רַשַּׁאי לְמֶחֱזֵי לֵיהּ. בָּכָה וְאִתְעַנִּי אַרְבְּעִין יוֹמִין אוֹחֲרָנִין, אַחֲזִיאוּ לֵיהּ בְּחֶזְוָוא לְרַבִּי שִׁמְעוֹן וְרַבִּי אֶלְעָזָר בְּרֵיהּ, דַּהֲווֹ לָעָאן בְּמִלָּה דָּא דַּאֲמַר רַבִּי יוֹסֵי, וְהֲווֹ כַּמָּה אַלְפִין צַיְיתִין לְמִלּוּלֵיהּ.

In his vision, Rav Chiya saw great celestial wings awaiting Rav Shimon and Rav Elazar. They mounted the wings, and they were borne aloft to the Heavenly Academy. Rav Chiya then saw that the splendor of Rav Shimon and Rav Elazar was constantly renewed, and they shone brighter than the sun.

51. אַדְהָכֵי, חֲמָא כַּמָּה גַּדְפִּין רַבְרְבִין עִלָּאִין, וְסַלִּיקוּ עֲלַיְיהוּ רַבִּי שִׁמְעוֹן וְרַבִּי אֶלְעָזָר בְּרֵיהּ וּסְלִיקוּ לִמְתִיבְתָּא דִּרְקִיעָא, וְכָל אִלֵּין גַּדְפִּין הֲווֹ מְחַכָּאן לְהוּ. חֲמָא דְּמִתְהַדְרָן וּמִתְחַדְּשָׁן בְּזִיווֹן וְנַהֲרוּ יַתִּיר מִנְּהוֹרָא דְּזִיוָא דְּשִׁמְשָׁא.

Rav Shimon opened the discussion by saying: "Let Rav Chiya enter and see how much the Holy One, blessed be He, shall restore the faces of the righteous in the world to come. How happy is he who comes here without shame, and how happy is he who stands erect in this world as a strong pillar that bears all!"

52. פָּתַח רַבִּי שִׁמְעוֹן וַאֲמַר, יֵיעוֹל רַבִּי חִיָּיא וְלֶיחֱמֵי, בְּכַמָּה דְּזַמִּין קֻדְשָׁא בְּרִיךְ הוּא לְחַדְּתָא אַנְפֵּי צַדִּיקַיָּיא לְזִמְנָא דְּאָתֵי. זַכָּאָה אִיהוּ מַאן דְּעָאל הָכָא בְּלָא כִּסּוּפָא וְזַכָּאָה מַאן דְּקָאֵים בְּהַהוּא עָלְמָא, כְּעַמּוּדָא תַּקִּיף בְּכֹלָּא, וְחֲמָא

Rav Chiya, in his vision, saw himself entering. He saw Rav Elazar stand up, as did all of the other pillars of the world, who had previously been seated. They all rose for the sake of Rav Chiya, and Rav Chiya felt unworthy. As he entered, he separated himself from the pillars of the world and sat at the feet of Rav Shimon.

דַּהֲוָה עָאל וַהֲוָה קָם רַבִּי אֶלְעָזָר וּשְׁאָר עַמּוּדִין דְּיָתְבִין תַּמָּן. וְהוּא הֲוָה כְּסִיף, וְאִשְׁתְּמִיט גַּרְמֵיהּ, וְעָאל וְיָתִיב לְרַגְלוֹי דְּרַבִּי שִׁמְעוֹן.

MEDITATION

Often a true yearning for connection with the Light comes only after an experience of pain and suffering. Through this meditation, yearning for the Light is awakened without a need for chaos in any aspect of our lives.

לְמֶחֱמֵי   יוֹמִין   אַרְבְּעִין   אִתְעַנִּי   יוֹמָא   מֵהַהוּא
lemechemei   yomin   arbein   itanei   yoma   mehahu

רַשָּׁאי   אַנְתְּ   לֵית   לֵיהּ   אֲמָרוּ   שִׁמְעוֹן   לְרִבִּי
rasha'ai   ant   leit   leih   amaru   Shimon   leRibbi

יוֹמִין   אַרְבְּעִין   וְאִתְעַנִּי   בָּכָה   לֵיהּ   לְמֶהֱוֵי
yomin   arbe'in   ve'itonei   becha   leih   lemehevei

שִׁמְעוֹן   לְרִבִּי   בְּחֶזְוָא   לֵיהּ   אַחֲזִיאוּ   אַחֲרִינִין,
Shimon   leRibbi   bechezva   leih   achaziu   acharinin

בְּרֵיהּ   אֶלְעָזָר   וְרִבִּי
bereih   Elazar   veRibbi

For forty days he fasted so that he might meet with Rav Shimon. When he was told, "You are not fit to see him," he wept and fasted for another forty days. Then, in a vision, he was shown Rav Shimon and Rav Elazar, his son.

When You Need to Remove Judgments From Your Life:

"Rav Yitzchak and the Power of Change"

(Zohar, Veyechi, verse 144)

Something in your life may seem both painful and beyond your power to change. It might be a problem in your work, or in your health, or in your relationship with someone close to you. But no matter how difficult or impossible a situation may appear—even if it seems like a sentence of death—any judgment can be removed through connection to the Light of the Creator.

Rav Yitzchak visits Rav Yehuda and speaks in a way that suggests that he, Rav Yitzchak, believes he is about to die. Rav Yehuda is disturbed by this, and asks Rav Yitzchak to explain. The two friends then decide to consult their teacher, Rav Shimon.

After seeing the Angel of Death in the presence of Rav Yitzchak, Rav Shimon asks God to withdraw this judgment—and the request is granted.

Rav Yitzchak then sleeps. He sees his father in a dream, who describes the welcome that had awaited Rav Yitzchak in heaven if he had died. But now Rav Yitzhak has gained a reprieve, until the day when he will enter the Upper World together with Rav Shimon.

One day Rav Yehuda was surprised to find Rav Yitzchak was sitting sadly at his door. Concerned, Rav Yehuda asked if anything was the matter.

144. ר' יִצְחָק, הֲוָה יָתֵיב יוֹמָא חַד, אַפִּתְחָא דְּר' יְהוּדָה, וַהֲוָה עָצִיב, נָפִיק ר' יְהוּדָה, אַשְׁכְּחֵיהּ לְתַרְעֵיהּ, דַּהֲוָה יָתֵיב וְעָצִיב, א'ל בַּאי יוֹמָא דֵּין מִשְׁאָר יוֹמִין.

Rav Yitzchak said, "I have come to ask three things of you. First, if you draw upon any of my teachings after I have left this world, be sure that you attribute them to me by name. Second, that you shall teach the Torah to my son, Yosef. Third, that you shall visit my grave during all the seven days of mourning, and if you have any requests, ask them there."

145. א'ל, אֲתֵינָא לְגַבָּךְ, לְמִבְעֵי מִינָךְ תְּלַת מִלִּין: חַד, דְּכַד תֵּימָא מִלֵּי דְּאוֹרַיְיתָא, וְתִדְכַּר מֵאִינוּן מִלִּין דַּאֲנָא אֲמֵינָא, דְּתֵימָא לוֹן בִּשְׁמִי, בְּגִין לְאַדְכָּרָא שְׁמִי. וְחַד דְּתִתְכֵּי לְיוֹסֵף בְּרִי בְּאוֹרַיְיתָא. וְחַד, דְּתֵיזִיל לְקִבְרִי כָּל ז' יוֹמִין, וְתִבְעֵי בָּעוּתִיךְ עָלַי.

Rav Yehuda replied, "From what you say, I see that you are expecting to die. But why do you believe this?" "My soul departs from me every night when I sleep," Rav Yitzchak told him, "but it no longer enlightens me with dreams. Moreover, when I pray and reach the verse, 'He who hears and accepts the prayers,' I then

146. א'ל מְנַן לָךְ. א'ל, הָא נִשְׁמָתִי אִסְתַּלְּקַת מִינִי בְּכָל לֵילְיָא, וְלָא אַנְהִיר לִי בְּחֶלְמָא, כְּמָה דַּהֲוָה בְּקַדְמֵיתָא, וְעוֹד דְּכַד אֲנָא מְצַלֵּינָא, וּמָטֵינָא לְשׁוֹמֵעַ תְּפִלָּה, אַשְׁגַּחְנָא בְּצוּלְמִי דִּילִי בְּכוֹתְלָא, וְלָא וָזמֵינָא לֵיהּ, וַאֲמֵינָא דְּהוֹאִיל וְצוּלְמָא אִתְעֲבַר וְלָא אִתְחֲזֵי, דְּהָא כָּרוֹזָא נָפִיק וְכָרֵיז,

look for my shadow upon the wall, but I do not see it. Then, because the shadow is gone I expect that I shall die. For it is written: 'Surely every man walks in a shadow.' As long as a man's shadow has not gone from him, 'every man walks.' That is, his spirit remains within him. But once a man's shadow is no longer seen, he passes away from this world."

Rav Yehuda added, "It is also derived from the verse, 'Because our days upon earth are a shadow.' Then Rav Yehuda said, "I shall carry out your requests. But I also ask that you shall reserve a place for me by you in the other world, as I was by your side in this world." Hearing this, Rav Yitzchak wept and said: "Please do not leave me alone."

They went to Rav Shimon and found him occupied with the Torah. Rav Shimon lifted up his eyes and saw the Angel of Death running and dancing before Rav Yitzchak.

דִּכְתִיב אַךְ בְּצֶלֶם יִתְהַלֶּךְ אִישׁ, כָּל זִמְנָא דְּצוּלְמָא דְּבַר נָשׁ לָא יִתְעֲבַר מִנֵּיהּ, יִתְהַלֶּךְ אִישׁ, וְרוּוְזֵיהּ אִתְקַיְּימָא בְּגַוֵּיהּ, אִתְעֲבַר צוּלְמָא דְּבַר נָשׁ וְלָא אִתְחֲזֵי, אִתְעֲבַר מֵהַאי עָלְמָא.

147. א'ל' וּמֵהָכָא, דִּכְתִיב כִּי צֵל יָמֵינוּ עֲלֵי אָרֶץ. א'ל', כָּל אִלֵּין מִלִּין דְּאַתְּ בָּעֵי עֲבִידְנָא, אֲבָל בָּעֵינָא מִינָךְ דְּבַהֲהוּא עָלְמָא, תְּבָרֵיר דּוּכְתָּאי גַּבָּךְ, כְּמָה דַּהֲוֵינָא בְּהַאי עָלְמָא. בָּכָה רִבִּי יִצְחָק וַאֲמַר, בִּמְטוּ מִינָךְ, דְּלָא תִתְפָּרַשׁ מִנָּאי כָּל אִלֵּין יוֹמִין.

148. אֲזָלוּ לְגַבֵּיהּ דְּרִבִּי שִׁמְעוֹן, אַשְׁכְּחוּהוּ דַּהֲוָה לָעֵי בְּאוֹרַיְיתָא, זָקִיף עֵינוֹי ר"ש, וְחָזְמָא לְרִבִּי יִצְחָק, וְחָזְמָא לְמַלְאַךְ הַמָּוֶת דְּרָהֵיט קַמֵּיהּ, וְרָקִיד קַמֵּיהּ.

Rav Shimon stood up, held Rav Yitzchak by the hand and said: "I decree that whoever is accustomed to come to me shall enter, and he who is not accustomed shall not come." Therefore the Angel of Death remained outside, unable to enter. But Rav Yitzchak and Rav Yehuda came in.

קָם רִבִּי שִׁמְעוֹן, אָוְזִיר בִּידֵיהּ דְּרִבִּי יִצְחָק, אָמַר, גּוֹזַרְנָא, מַאן דְּרָגִיל לְמֵיעַל, יֵיעוֹל. וּמַאן דְּלָא רָגִיל לְמֵיעָאל, לָא יֵיעוֹל. עָאלוּ רִבִּי יִצְחָק וְרִבִּי יְהוּדָה, קָטֵיר מַלְאַךְ הַמָּוֶת לְבַר.

Rav Shimon looked at Rav Yitzchak, and saw that his time to die would not come until the eighth hour of the day. Rav Shimon said to his son, Rav Elazar: "Sit at the door, and whoever you see, do not speak with him. If he shall want to enter, invoke an oath that he may not enter." Then Rav Shimon placed Rav Yitzchak before him, and studied the Torah with him.

149. אַשְׁגַּח ר"ש, וְזָמְנָא, דְּעַד כְּעַן לָא מְטָא עִדָנָא, דְּהָא עַד תְּמַנְיָא שַׁעֲתֵי דְּיוֹמָא הֲוָה זִמְנָא, אוֹתְבֵיהּ קַמֵּי ר"ש, וַהֲוָה לָעֵי לֵיהּ בְּאוֹרַיְיתָא. אר"ש לְרִבִּי אֶלְעָזָר בְּרֵיהּ, תִּיב אַפִּתְחָא וּמַה דְּתֶחֱמֵי, לָא תִשְׁתָּעֵי בַּהֲדֵיהּ, וְאִי יִבְעֵי לְמֵיעָאל הָכָא, אוֹמֵי אוֹמָאָה דְּלָא לֵיעוֹל.

Rav Shimon said to Rav Yitzchak: "Have you seen the image of your departed father today, or have you not seen it? For we have learned that when a man is about to depart from the world, his father and relatives who have passed away are there with him, and he sees and recognizes them.

150. אָמַר ר"ש לְרִבִּי יִצְחָק, וְזָמֵית דְּיוֹקְנָא דַּאֲבוּךְ יוֹמָא דָא, אוֹ לָא. דְּהָא, תָּנֵינָן, בְּשַׁעֲתָא דְּבַר נָשׁ אִסְתַּלָּק מֵעַלְמָא, אֲבוּי וּקְרִיבוֹי מִשְׁתַּכְּחִין תַּמָּן עִמֵּיהּ, וְזָמְנָא לוֹן, וְאִשְׁתְּמוֹדַע לוֹן, וְכָל אִינוּן דַּהֲוָה מְדוֹרֵיהּ גַּבַּיְיהוּ בְּהַהוּא

And all those with whom he will dwell in the other world gather to be with him, and accompany his soul to its dwelling place." Rav Yitzchak replied: "Until now I have not seen the image of my father."

עַלְמָא בְּדַרְגָּא וַזַד, כֻּלְהוּ מִתְכַּנְּשֵׁי וּמִשְׁתַּכְחֵי עֲמֵיהּ, וְאָזְלִין עִם נִשְׁמָתֵיהּ, עַד אֲתַר דְּתִשְׁרֵי בְּאַתְרֵיהּ. אֲמַר, עַד כְּעַן לָא וָזֵמִינָא.

Then Rav Shimon stood up and said: "Master of the universe, we have a certain Rav Yitzchak with us, who is one of the seven eyes. Behold, as I hold him now, give Him to me!" A voice resounded saying: "The throne of His Master, has approached union on the wings of Rav Shimon. Behold, Rav Yitzchak is yours, and you shall come with him when you yourself shall sit in your place." Rav Shimon said, "Certainly, I shall bring him with me when I depart from the world."

151. אַדְהֲכֵי קָם ר שִׁמְעוֹן וַאֲמַר, מָארֵי דְעָלְמָא, אִשְׁתְּמוֹדַע רִבִּי יִצְחָק לְגַבָּן, וּמֵאִנּוּן שִׁבְעָה עַיְינִין דְּהָכָא הוּא, הָא אֲחִזְנָא בֵּיהּ, וְהַב לִי. נָפַק קָלָא וַאֲמַר, כּוּרְסְיָיא דְּמָארֵיהּ קָרִיבָא בְּגַדְפוֹי דְּר שִׁמְעוֹן, הָא דִּידָךְ הוּא, וְעִמָּךְ תַּיְיתֵיהּ, בְּזִימְנָא דְּתֵיעוֹל לְמִשְׁרֵי בְּכוּרְסְיָךְ. אֲמַר ר"ע וַדַּאי.

While Rav Shimon was speaking, Rav Elazar saw the Angel of Death depart and Rav Elazar said: "No judgment stands at the place of Rav Shimon." Rav Shimon then said to Rav Elazar: "Come here and hold Rav Yitzchak, for I see he is afraid." Rav

152. אַדְהֲכֵי, וְזָמָא רִבִּי אֶלְעָזָר, דַּהֲוָה אִסְתְּלִיק מַלְאָךְ הַמָּוֶת, וַאֲמַר, לֵית קוּפְטְרָא דְּטִיפְסָא, בַּאֲתַר דְּרִבִּי שִׁמְעוֹן בֶּן יוֹחָאי שְׁכִיחַ. אֲמַר רִבִּי שִׁמְעוֹן לְרִבִּי אֶלְעָזָר בְּרֵיהּ, עוֹל הָכָא, וְאָחֵיד בֵּיהּ בְּרִבִּי יִצְחָק,

Elazar entered and held him, and Rav Shimon turned to study the Torah.

דְּהָא וְזָמֵינָא בֵּיהּ דִּמְסתַּפֵּי, עָאל רִבִּי אֶלְעָזָר, וְאָחֵיד בֵּיהּ. וְרִבִּי שִׁמְעוֹן אַהֲדַר אַנְפֵּיהּ וְכָעֵי בְּאוֹרַיְיתָא.

Then Rav Yitzchak slept, and in a dream he saw his father. His father said to him: "My son, happy is your portion in this world and in the World to Come, for you sit among the leaves of The Tree of Life in the Garden of Eden. A great and strong tree in both worlds is Rav Shimon. He holds you in his boughs. Happy is your portion, my son."

153. נָיֵים רִבִּי יִצְחָק, וְחָמָא לְאָבוֹי, א'ל' בְּרִי, זַכָּאָה וְחוּלָקָךְ, בְּעַלְמָא דֵּין, וּבְעַלְמָא דְּאָתֵי, דְּהָא בֵּין טַרְפֵּי אִילָנָא דְחַיֵּי דְּגִנְתָא דְעֵדֶן, אִתְיְהֵיב אִילָנָא רַבָּא וְתַקִּיף בִּתְרֵין עָלְמִין, ר'ש' בֶּן יוֹחָאי הוּא, דְּהָא הוּא אָחֵיד לָךְ בְּעַנְפּוֹי, זַכָּאָה וְחוּלָקָךְ בְּרִי.

Rav Yitzchak asked, "Father, what will be my place there, in the World of Truth?" And Rav Yitzchak's father said to him: "For three days your chamber has been prepared, with open windows to shine upon you from the four directions of the world. I had seen your place, I had rejoiced and said: 'Happy is your portion, son.' The only thing that saddened me was the fact that your son had not yet studied Torah."

154. אֲמַר לֵיהּ אַבָּא, וּמַה אֲנָא הָתַם, אֲמַר לֵיהּ תְּלַת יוֹמִין הֲווֹ דְּוַזְפוּ אַדְרָא דְמַשְׁכְּבָךְ, וְתַקִּינוּ לָךְ כֵּיוָן פְּתִיחָן, לְאַנְהָרָא לָךְ מֵאַרְבַּע סִטְרִין דְּעַלְמָא, וַאֲנָא וָזְמֵינָא דּוּכְתָּיךְ וְחָדֵינָא, דַּאֲמֵינָא זַכָּאָה וְחוּלָקָךְ בְּרִי. בַּר דְּעַד כְּעַן, בְּרָךְ לָא זָכֵי בְּאוֹרַיְיתָא.

Rav Yitzchak's father continued: "Twelve righteous men from among the friends were preparing to go to you. As they were going, a sound went forth in all the worlds: 'Friends who stand here, Rav Shimon has asked a request of the Holy One, blessed be He, that Rav Yitzchak shall not die! And the request has been granted!'

"Not only this, but seventy places are adorned for Rav Shimon in the Upper World. Each place has doors opening to seventy worlds, each world opening to seventy channels, each opened for seventy supernal crowns, where there are ways leading to Atika,' the most concealed of all, to see the highest pleasantness which delights and shines upon all, as it says: 'to behold the pleasantness of God, and to inquire in His temple.' As it is written: 'For he is the trusted one in all my house.'"

Rav Yitzchak asked, "Father, how long am I given to live in this world?" His father

155. וְהָא הַשְׁתָּא הֲוֵי זְמִינִין לְמֵיתֵי גַּבָּךְ, תְּרֵיסַר צַדִּיקַיָּא דְּחַבְרַיָּא, וְעַד דַּהֲוֵינָא נָפְקֵי, אִתְּעַר קָלָא בְּכֻלְּהוּ עָלְמִין, מַאן וַזְבְּרִין דְּקָיְימִין הָכָא, אִתְעֲטָרוּ, בְּגִינֵיהּ דְּרִבִּי שִׁמְעוֹן, שְׁאֶלְתָּא שָׁאֵיל, וְאִתְיְיהִיב לֵיהּ.

156. וְלָא דָא בִּלְחוֹדוֹי, דְּהָא שַׁבְעִין דּוּכְתֵּי מִתְעַטְּרָן הָכָא דִּילֵיהּ. וְכָל דּוּכְתָּא וְדוּכְתָּא, פְּתִיחִין פְּתִיחִין לְשַׁבְעִין עָלְמִין, וְכָל עָלְמָא וְעָלְמָא, אִתְפַּתְּחוּ לֵיהּ רְהִיטִין, וְכָל רְהִיטָא וּרְהִיטָא, אִתְפַּתְּחוּ לְשַׁבְעִין כִּתְרִין עִלָּאִין, וּמִתַּמָּן אִתְפַּתְּחוּ אָרְחִין לְעַתִּיקָא, סְתִימָאָה דְּכֹלָּא, לְמֶחֱמֵי בְּהַהוּא נְעִימוּתָא עִלָּאָה דְּנָהֲרָא, וּמְהַנְיָא לְכֹלָּא, כְּמָה דְּאַתְּ אָמֵר, לַחֲזוֹת בְּנֹעַם ה' וּלְבַקֵּר בְּהֵיכָלוֹ, מַהוּ וּלְבַקֵּר בְּהֵיכָלוֹ, הַיְינוּ דִּכְתִיב בְּכָל בֵּיתִי נֶאֱמָן הוּא.

157. אֲמַר לֵיהּ אַבָּא, כַּמָּה זִמְנָא יְהִיבוּ לִי בְּהַאי עָלְמָא.

replied, "I was not given permission to tell you this, for man is not made to know it. But at the feast for Rav Shimon on the day of his departure, you shall be there to set his table and to reveal mysteries with him. As it is written, 'Go forth, O daughters of Zion, and behold King Solomon with the crown with which his mother crowned him on the day of his wedding, and on the day of the gladness of his heart.'"

א'ל לֵית לִי רְשׁוּתָא, וְלָא מוֹדְעֵי לֵיהּ לְבַר נָשׁ, אֲבָל בְּהִלּוּלָא רַבָּא דר' שִׁמְעוֹן, תְּהֵא מְתַקֵּן פָּתוּרֵיהּ, כד'א צְאֶינָה וּרְאֶינָה בְּנוֹת צִיּוֹן בַּמֶּלֶךְ שְׁלֹמֹה בַּעֲטָרָה שֶׁעִטְּרָה לּוֹ אִמּוֹ בְּיוֹם חֲתֻנָתוֹ וּבְיוֹם שִׂמְחַת לִבּוֹ.

Rav Yitzchak then awoke and laughed and his face shone. Rav Shimon looked at his face and said: "You have heard a great revelation." Rav Yitzchak replied, "Surely I have heard." He told Rav Shimon what he had seen in his dream, and he prostrated himself on the ground before Rav Shimon.

158. אַדְהָכֵי אִתְעַר רְבִּי יִצְחָק, וַהֲוָה חָיֵיךְ, וְאַנְפּוֹי נְהִירִין, וְחָמָא רְבִּי שִׁמְעוֹן, וְאִסְתְּכַל בְּאַנְפּוֹי, א'ל מִלָּה חַדְתָּא שְׁמַעְתָּא, אָמַר לֵיהּ וַדַּאי, סָח לֵיהּ, אִשְׁתַּטַּח קַמֵּיהּ דְּרְבִּי שִׁמְעוֹן.

We have learned that, from that day onward, Rav Yitzchak took his son's hand, and he studied the Torah with his son, and never left him. When he came before

159. תָּאנָא, מֵהַהוּא יוֹמָא, הֲוָה רְבִּי יִצְחָק אָחֵיד לִבְרֵיהּ בִּידֵיהּ, וְלָעֵי לֵיהּ בְּאוֹרַיְיתָא, וְלָא הֲוָה שַׁבְקֵיהּ.

Rav Shimon, his son would sit outside. Rav Yitzchak would sit before Rav Shimon and declare: "O God remove my pain and be my protection."

כַּד הֲוָה עָאל קַמֵּיהּ דְּרִבִּי
שִׁמְעוֹן, אוֹתְבֵיהּ לִבְרֵיהּ לְבַר,
וְיָתִיב קַמֵּיהּ דְּרִבִּי שִׁמְעוֹן,
וַהֲוָה קָרֵי קַמֵּיהּ ה' עָשְׂקָה לִּי
עָרְבֵנִי.

MEDITATION

Reading this section and using the meditation can awaken the energy to remove judgments. Just as Rav Shimon removed the judgment of death that was upon Rav Yitzchak, we can gain the power to remove negative decrees.

אַדְהָכֵי, וְזָמָא רִבִּי אֶלְעָזָר, דַּהֲוָה אִסְתַּלֵּיק
istalek dahavah Elazar Ribbi chama adhachei

מַלְאָךְ הַמָּוֶת, וַאֲמַר, לֵית קוּפְטְרָא דְּטִיפְסָא,
detifsa koftera leit va'amar hamavet malach

בַּאֲתַר דְּרִבִּי שִׁמְעוֹן בֶּן יוֹחַאי שְׁכִיחַ.
shechi'ach Yochai ben Shimon deRibbi ba'atar

While Rav Shimon was speaking, Rav Elazar saw the Angel of Death depart and Rav Elazar said: "No judgment stands at the place of Rav Shimon."

161

A Place Beyond Death:

"The channel of immortality"

(Zohar, Trumah, verse 467)

Almost everyone fears death. Though death seems inevitable and beyond our control, Kabbalah teaches that this is not so. The world as we now know it is not the ultimate state of being. Death is necessary at this point, but ultimately there will be immortality, and this will be brought about by our spiritual work. Unlike other spiritual goals that we can reach individually, immortality can only be brought about when a critical mass has been achieved and transformation takes place throughout humankind.

The Zohar reveals that there is a location in the world where the angel of destruction has no dominion: Death does not exist there. The letter *Tet*, which is a channel for endless life, is suspended over that place and because of the energy of that letter, death has no power in that location. The destroying angel cannot enter there, and he flees from the letter *Tet*. The physical location of this place is unimportant. It is not a magical Shangri-La that we should search for; rather, it is a physical location that represents a seed of consciousness that can later blossom into a global consciousness that immortality is possible. After asking Rav Yitzchak for an explanation of this, the students approach Rav Shimon. Rav Shimon explains that God created the world using the energies of the Hebrew letters and the engravings of the Holy Name. As the kabbalists teach, the Hebrew letters and language are a universal means of communication. They are forms through which all humankind can connect to the Light of the Creator.

The spiritual work of bringing immortality to the world has already been started for us. God has planted the seed of immortality through the creation of a place where there is no death. This is an open line—a channel—to the energy of immortality. Because of this seed, we are not called upon to create something from nothing. Instead, we have the much easier task of expanding a channel that already exists.

To do this, we don't need to search for or go to the physical place of immortality. Instead, our spiritual work should be to connect with the energy of immortality, and with the "death of death," which is our true destiny.

In this section, it's important to understand why Rav Yitzchak declines to comment when he's asked why the angel of death has no dominion. Rav Yitzchak does not speak because he himself was never taught this by his teachers. As a kabbalist, Rav Yitzchak would never speak about something in which he had not been instructed. Instead, the question is taken to the higher authority of Rav Shimon.

There is a place in the world where the angel of destruction and death has no dominion and is not permitted to enter. Those who live there do not die until they go out of the city. There is not one there who does not die. They die elsewhere, like other people, but not in the city. What is the reason that they die? They cannot always remain in the city. Rather, they come and go, and therefore they all die.

What is the reason that the destroying angel has no dominion there? If you say that the city is not in his domain, behold, the Holy Land is also not in his domain, but people still die there. So what is the reason people do not die in this place? If you say it is because of the holiness of the place, behold, there is no place that is holy like the Land of Israel, but people still die there. And if you say it is because of the merit of the man who built the city, behold there were many people who merited more

467. אֲתַר אִית בְּיִשׁוּבָא, דְּלָא שַׁלְטָא בֵּיהּ הַהוּא מְחַבְּלָא, וְלָא אִתְיְהִיב לֵיהּ רְשׁוּ לְאַעֲלָא תַּמָּן, וְכָל אִינוּן דְּדַיְירֵי תַּמָּן, לָא מֵתִין, עַד דְּנָפְקִין לְבַר מִקַּרְתָּא. וְלֵית לָךְ בַּר נָשׁ מִכָּל דְּדַיְירִין תַּמָּן, דְּלָא מֵתִין, וְכֻלְּהוּ מֵתִין כִּשְׁאַר בְּנֵי נָשָׁא, אֲבָל לָאו בְּמָתָא. מ"ט. בְּגִין דְּלָא יַכְלִין לְמֵיתַב תָּדִיר בְּמָתָא, אֶלָּא אִלֵּין נָפְקִין, וְאִלֵּין עָאלִין, וְע"ד כֻּלְּהוּ מֵתִין.

468. מ"ט לָא שַׁלְטָא תַּמָּן הַהוּא מַלְאָךְ מְחַבְּלָא. אִי תֵּימָא דְּלָא קָיְימָא בִּרְשׁוּתֵיהּ, הָא אַרְעָא קַדִּישָׁא דְּלָא קַיְימָא בִּרְשׁוּ אַחֲרָא, וּמֵתִין, בְּהַהוּא אֲתַר אֲמַאי לָא מֵתִין. אִי תֵּימָא בְּגִין קְדוּשָׁא, לֵית אֲתַר בִּקְדוּשָׁה בְּכָל יִשׁוּבָא כְּגַוְונָא דְּאֶרֶץ יִשְׂרָאֵל. וְאִי תֵּימָא, בְּגִין הַהוּא גַּבְרָא דְּבָנֵי לָהּ. כַּמָּה בְּנֵי נָשָׁא הֲווֹ דִּזְכֻוּתֵיהוֹן יַתִּיר מִדִּילֵיהּ. אָמַר רַבִּי יִצְחָק, אֲנָא לָא שְׁמַעְנָא וְלָא אֵימָא.

than him. Rav Yitzchak said, "I did not hear anything from my teachers about this, and I cannot comment."

They came and asked Rav Shimon. He said to them, "Certainly the Angel of Death has no dominion over that place, and God does not want any person to ever die there. If you say people did die in that place originally before the city was built, it is not so. From the day that man was created, that place was established, and the secret of secrets is contained in this idea, for those who view the secrets of Wisdom.

469. אָתוּ שָׁאִילוּ לֵיהּ לְר'יע, אָמַר לוֹן, וַדַּאי הַהוּא אֲתָר לָא שַׁלְטָא עֲלֵיהּ מַלְאָךְ הַמָּוֶת, וְקוּדְשָׁא בְּרִיךְ הוּא לָא בָּעֵי דִּבְהַהוּא אֲתָר יְמוּת בַּר נָשׁ לְעָלְמִין, וְאִי תֵימָא, דִּקֹדֶם לָכֵן בְּהַהוּא דּוּכְתָּא, עַד לָא אִתְבְּנֵי, מִיתוּ בֵּיהּ בְּנֵי נָשָׁא, לָאו הָכִי. אֶלָּא מִיּוֹמָא דְּאִתְבְּרֵי עָלְמָא, אִתְתַּקָּן הַהוּא אֲתָר, לְקַיּוֹמָא, וְרָזָא דְרָזִין הָכָא, לְאִינוּן דְּמִסְתַּכְּלֵי בְּרָזָא דְּחָכְמְתָא.

"When God created the world, He created it with the secret of the letters of the Hebrew alphabet. The letters began to spin, from the last letter toward the first, and He created the world with the engravings of the Holy Name, and the letters spun and surrounded the world with engravings. When the world became manifest, when it expanded and was created,

470. כַּד בָּרָא קוּדְשָׁא בְּרִיךְ הוּא עָלְמָא, בָּרָא לֵיהּ בְּרָזָא דְּאַתְוָון, וְאִתְגַּלְגְּלוּ אַתְוָון, וּבָרָא עָלְמָא, בְּגִלּוּפֵי דִשְׁמָא קַדִּישָׁא. אִתְגַּלְגְּלוּ אַתְוָון, וְאִסְתַּחֲרוּ עָלְמָא בְּגִלּוּפֵי וְכַד אִתְגְּלֵי וְאִתְפָּשַׁט עָלְמָא וְאִתְבְּרֵי, וַהֲווּ אַתְוָון סַחֲרָן לְמִבְרֵי, אָמַר קוּדְשָׁא בְּרִיךְ הוּא דְּיִסְתַּיֵּים בְּיּוֹ"ד,

and the letters were circling to create, God said that the world should be concluded with *Yud,* the tenth letter. The letter *Tet,* the ninth letter, remained suspended in the air in that place, where the destroying angel would have no dominion. *Tet* is the letter that illuminates with life; therefore, it is a good sign for anyone who sees the letter *Tet* in a dream, and life is prepared for him. Therefore, since *Tet* is suspended over that place, death has no dominion there."

אִשְׁתְּאָרַת אָת ט׳ בְּהַהוּא דּוּכְתָּא, תַּלְיָא בַּאֲוִירָא, טַ״ת, אִיהוּ אָת, דְּנָהִירוּ וַחַיִּין, בְּגִין כָּךְ, מַאן דְּחָמֵי טַ״ת בְּחֶלְמֵיה, סִימָנָא טָבָא הוּא לֵיה, וְחַיִּין אִתְתַּקָּנוּ לֵיה. וְעַל דָּא בְּגִין דַּהֲוָה ט׳ תַּלְיָא עַל גַּבֵּי הַהוּא אֲתָר, לָא שַׁלְטָא בֵּיה מוֹתָא.

MEDITATION

Reading this section awakens understanding that the channel of immortality exists and keeps us focused on immortality not only as the goal of our work, but as our true destiny.

אֲתָר אִית בִּישׁוּבָא,   דְּלָא שַׁלְטָא בֵּיהּ הַהוּא
hahu beih shalta dela beyishuva   it atar

מְחַבְּלָא,   וְלָא אִתְיְיהִיב לֵיהּ רְשׁוּ לְאַעֲלָא תַּמָּן
taman le'a'ala reshu leih ityehiv vela mechabla

There is no greater reward in the world than to study Torah. And payment for this study is not necessary, as it is written, "Gold and crystal cannot equal it; and the exchange of it shall not be for vessels of fine gold."

Assistance From the Souls

of the Righteous:

"The passing of Rav Shimon"

(Zohar, Haazinu, verse 196)

Life brings many situations that we simply can't handle alone. We need help, and Kabbalah offers wisdom for facing life's challenges. But beyond understanding, Kabbalah also provides practical tools. One of these is the power to gain the assistance of the souls of the righteous who have departed this world. This can be accomplished by visiting the graves of righteous people, and also by studying their teachings. The kabbalists further explain that, when a righteous person dies, it is at the moment of death that his or her full Light is revealed.

This section of the Zohar describes the final moments of Rav Shimon's life, at the conclusion of the *Idra Zuta* (the smaller assembly). It speaks of the appreciation for Rav Shimon that was felt by everyone around him. Respect for him was so great that there were violent arguments about where he should be buried. By reading this section, we connect to the ultimate level of the soul of Rav Shimon.

Rav Aba said, "Rav Shimon had barely finished uttering the word 'life' when his words ceased. I was writing down his words, and was about to write more, yet I heard nothing. I did not raise my head, because the Light was great and I could not look. I then trembled and heard a voice calling and saying, 'Length of days, and long life...' Then I heard another voice saying, 'He asked life of You...'

"All that day the fire did not cease from the house, and no one could reach him, because of the Light and fire that encircled him. I was prostrate on the ground all that day, crying loudly. After the fire was gone, I saw that Rav Shimon — the Holy Light, the Holy of Holies — had departed from the world, and was lying on his right side with a smiling face.

"Rav Elazar, his son, rose and took his hands and kissed them, while I kissed the dust beneath his feet. The friends started crying. Rav Elazar fell to the ground

196. א'ר אַבָּא, לָא סַיֵּים בּוֹצִינָא קַדִּישָׁא לְמֵימַר וַיַּים, עַד דְּאִשְׁתְּכָכוּ מִלּוֹי, וַאֲנָא כַּתַבְנָא, סָבַרְנָא לְמִכְתַּב טְפַי, וְלָא שְׁמַעְנָא. וְלָא זְקִיפְנָא רֵישָׁא, דִּנְהוֹרָא הֲוָה סַגִּי, וְלָא הֲוָה יְכִילְנָא לְאִסְתַּכְּלָא. אַדְהָכִי אוֹזְדַעְזַעְנָא, שְׁמַעְנָא קָלָא דְּקָארֵי וְאָמַר אֶרֶךְ יָמִים וּשְׁנוֹת וַיַּים וְגוֹ'. שְׁמַעְנָא קָלָא אָחֳרָא, וַיַּים שָׁאַל מִמְּךָ וְגוֹ'.

197. כֹּל הַהוּא יוֹמָא, לָא אַפְסִיק אֶשָּׁא מִן בֵּיתָא, וְלָא הֲוָה מַאן דְּמָטֵי לְגַבֵּיה, דְּלָא יְכִילוּ דִּנְהוֹרָא וְאֶשָּׁא הֲוָה בְּסוֹחֲרָנֵיה. כֹּל הַהוּא יוֹמָא נָפִילְנָא עַל אַרְעָא, וְגָעֵינָא. בָּתַר דְּאָזִיל אֶשָּׁא, וַחֲמֵינָא לְבוּצִינָא קַדִּישָׁא קֹדֶשׁ הַקֳדָשִׁים, דְּאִסְתַּלַּק מִן עָלְמָא, אִתְעֲטָּף שָׁכִיב עַל יְמִינֵיה, וְאַנְפּוֹי וַיְיכִין.

198. קָם רַבִּי אֶלְעָזָר בְּרֵיה, וְנָטִיל יְדוֹי וְנָשִׁיק לוֹן, וַאֲנָא לַחֲכִנָא עַפְרָא דִּתְחוֹת רַגְלוֹי. בָּעוּ וַחַבְרַיָּיא לְמִבְכֵּי, וְלָא יְכִילוּ לְמַלְלָא.

three times, and could not open his mouth. At last he said: 'Father, father, there were three that became one again.' Now, after this great tree is gone, the beasts that used to walk under the tree will wander, and the birds that used to dwell in its boughs will sink into the chasm in the great sea, and the friends, instead of the good they received from the tree, will drink blood."

שָׁארוּ וַזבְרַיָּא בִּבְכִיָה, וְרִבִּי אֶלְעָזָר בְּרֵיה נָפִיל תְּלַת זִמְנִין, וְלָא יָכִיל לְמִפְתַּח פּוּמֵיה. לְבָתַר פָּתַח וְאָמַר, אַבָּא אַבָּא. תְּלָת הֲווֹ, וַד אִתְחֲזָרוּ. הַשְׁתָּא תְּנוּד וֵיוָתָא, צִפְרָאן טָאסִין, מִשְׁתַּקְעָן בְּנוּקְבָּאן דְּיַמָּא רַבָּא, וְחַבְרַיָּא כֻּלְּהוּ שַׁתְיִין דָּמָא.

Rav Chiya rose and said: "Until now the Holy Light protected us. Now is the time to strive to honor him." Rav Elazar and Rav Aba rose and took Rav Shimon to a bed made like a ladder. Who has ever seen such confusion of the friends! The whole house emitted good fragrances. They raised him on his bed, and none served him but Rav Elazar and Rav Aba.

199. קָם רִבִּי וַזַּיָּא עַל רַגְלוֹי וְאָמַר, עַד הַשְׁתָּא בּוּצִינָא קַדִּישָׁא מִסְתַּכַּל עֲלָן. הַשְׁתָּא לָאו הוּא עִדָּן, אֶלָּא לְאִשְׁתַּדְּלָא בִּיקָרֵיה. קָם רִבִּי אֶלְעָזָר וְר אַבָּא, נַטְלוּ לֵיה בְּטִיקְרָא דְּסִיקְלָא, מַאן חָזָא עִרְבּוּבְיָא דַחַבְרַיָּא, וְכָל בֵּיתָא הֲוָה סָלִיק רֵיחִין סְלִיקוּ בֵּיה בְּפוּרְיֵיה, וְלָא אִשְׁתַּמֵּשׁ בֵּיה, אֶלָּא ר אֶלְעָזָר וְר אַבָּא.

Thugs and armed men came from the village of Tzipori, wanting him to be buried there. The inhabitants of Meron drove them away and shouted at them in their

200. אָתוּ טְרִיקִין, וּמָארֵי תְּרִיסִין דִּכְפַר צִפּוֹרִי וְטַרְדָּא בְּהוּ בְּנֵי מִרוֹנְיָא, צֵוְוחִין בִּקְטִירִין, דְּלָא יִתְקְבַר תַּמָּן.

170

multitudes, because they wanted him to be buried where they themselves lived. After his bed was taken from the house, it rose in the air and fire burned before it. Then a voice said, "Come and gather to the celebration of Rav Shimon. Let him come in peace and rest in his resting place."

בָּתַר דְּנָפַק פּוּרְיָיא, הֲוָה סָלִיק בַּאֲוִירָא. וְאֶשָּׁא הֲוָה לָהִיט קַמֵּיהּ, שָׁמְעוּ קָלָא, עוּלוּ וְאָתוּ, וְאִתְכְּנָשׁוּ לְהִילּוּלָא דְּרִבִּי שִׁמְעוֹן, יָבֹא שָׁלוֹם יָנוּחוּ עַל מִשְׁכְּבוֹתָם.

When Rav Shimon entered the cave, they heard a voice from inside: "This is the man who caused the earth to tremble, who caused kingdoms to tremble. How many prosecuting angels in the heavens are quieted today for your sake! This is Rav Shimon bar Yochai, with whom his Master glorifies Himself daily. Blessed is his portion above and below. How many supernal treasures await him! Of him it says, 'And you should go to the end and rest, and stand up for your allotted portion at the end of the days.'"

201. כַּד עָאל לִמְעַרְתָּא שָׁמְעוּ קָלָא בִּמְעַרְתָּא, זֶה הָאִישׁ מַרְעִישׁ הָאָרֶץ מַרְגִּיז מַמְלָכוֹת, כַּמָּה פִּטְרִין בִּרְקִיעָא מִשְׁתַּכְּכִין בְּיוֹמָא דֵין בְּגִינָךְ, דְּנָא רעב"י, דְּמָארֵיהּ מִשְׁתַּבַּח בֵּיהּ בְּכָל יוֹמָא. זַכָּאָה חוּלָקֵיהּ לְעֵילָא וְתַתָּא. כַּמָּה גְּנִיזִין עִלָּאִין מִסְתַּמְרָן לֵיהּ, עֲלֵיהּ אִתְּמַר וְאַתָּה לֵךְ לַקֵּץ וְתָנוּחַ וְתַעֲמֹד לְגוֹרָלְךָ לְקֵץ הַיָּמִין.

MEDITATION

With this meditation, we connect to the great soul of Rav Shimon bar Yochai and draw his assistance to our lives when we need it.

זֶה הָאִישׁ מַרְעִישׁ הָאָרֶץ מַרְגִּיז מַמְלָכוֹת,
mamlachot margiz ha'aretz marish ha'ish zeh

כַּמָּה פִּטְרִין בִּרְקִיעָא מִשְׁתַּכְּכִין בְּיוֹמָא
beyoma mishtakechin birki'a pitrin kamah

דֵּין בְּגִינָךְ, דְּנָא רשב"י, דִּמָארֵיהּ
demareih Ribbi Shimon Bar Yochai dena beginach dein

מִשְׁתַּבַּח בֵּיהּ בְּכָל יוֹמָא. זַכָּאָה חוּלָקֵיהּ
chulakei zaka'ah yoma bechol beih mishtebach

לְעֵילָא וְתַתָּא. כַּמָּה גְּנִיזִין עִלָּאִין מִסְתַּמְרָן
mistamran ila'in genizin kamah vetata le'eila

לֵיהּ, עֲלֵיהּ אִתְּמַר וְאַתָּה לֵךְ לַקֵּץ וְתָנוּחַ
vetanuach laketz lech vetatah itmar aleih leih

וְתַעֲמוֹד לְגוֹרָלְךָ לְקֵץ הַיָּמִין.
hayamin leketz legoralcha veta'amod

This is the man who caused the earth to tremble, who caused kingdoms to tremble. How many prosecuting angels in the heavens are quieted today for your sake! This is Rav Shimon bar Yochai, with whom his Master glorifies Himself daily. Blessed is his portion above and below. How many supernal treasures await him! Of him it says, 'And you should go to the end and rest, and stand up for your allotted portion at the end of the days.'

THE SOURCE OF ALL TRUE

FULFILLMENT:

"RAV ABA AND RAV YOSI"

(ZOHAR, LECH LECHA, VERSE 282)

Right now, what are you looking forward to in your life? Maybe it's a better job or an exciting relationship. You might be hoping for a vacation in Hawaii, a summer home on Cape Cod, or a thousand other varieties of "more," "different," and "better." Don't feel at all guilty about this. In fact, Kabbalah teaches that we should enjoy what the physical world has to offer—but we should also know that nothing in the physical world can bring us truly lasting fulfillment.

Whenever you feel joy in anything, the true source of that enjoyment is the spark of the Creator's Light that is present there. Even when you take a bite of chocolate, the pleasure you feel is actually the Light, because there's a spark of Light in all physical things. But the pleasure is only momentary, because it's just a spark of Light. It's only through our spiritual work that we can connect to the infinite abundance of Light that brings complete and lasting fulfillment.

This section of the Zohar speaks of Torah study, or spiritual work, which is much more than an intellectual experience. Torah study reveals enormous Light, both to the individual student and to the world. Our motivation for study should not be selfish desire for knowledge. Study should be for the purpose of revealing Light for ourselves and imparting it to others.

This section concerns the Light that is revealed through Torah study (spiritual work). Rav Aba helps his student, Rav Yosi, transform his spiritual work from a selfish pursuit to a process of connection to the Light of the Creator, all for the betterment of Rav Yosi's life and for the world as a whole.

After Rav Aba returned from Babylon, he declared that whoever desired wealth and eternal life in the World to Come should study Torah; and the entire community gathered around him to study. In the neighborhood there was a certain bachelor. One day he said to Rav Aba: "Rav, I wish to learn Torah so that I may be wealthy." Rav Aba responded, "Why, of course. You shall merit much wealth by studying Torah. What is your name?" The bachelor responded, "Yosi." Then Rav Aba told his students to refer the bachelor as, "Yosi, a man of great wealth and glory." And Yosi undertook to study Torah.

282. ר אַבָּא כַּד אָתָא מֵהָתָם, הֲוָה מַכְרִיז, מַאן בָּעֵי עוֹתְרָא, וּמַאן בָּעֵי אוֹרְכָא דְּחַיֵּי בְּעָלְמָא דְאָתֵי, יֵיתֵי וְיִשְׁתַּדַּל בְּאוֹרַיְיתָא. הֲווֹ מִתְכַּנְּשִׁין כּוּלֵי עָלְמָא לְגַבֵּיהּ. רַוָּוק חַד הֲוָה בְּשִׁיבְבוּתֵיהּ. יוֹמָא חַד אָתָא לְגַבֵּיהּ, אָמַר לוֹ ר, בָּעֵינָא לְמִלְעֵי בְּאוֹרַיְיתָא, כְּדֵי שֶׁיְּהֵא לִי עוֹתְרָא. אָמַר לוֹ הָא וַדַּאי. אָמַר לוֹ מַה שְׁמָךְ. אָמַר לוֹ יוֹסֵי. אָמַר לוֹן לְתַלְמִידוֹי דְּיִקְרוֹן לֵיהּ ר יוֹסֵי מָארֵי דְעוֹתְרָא וִיקָרָא. יָתִיב וְאִתְעַסַּק בְּאוֹרַיְיתָא.

Time passed. One day Yosi stood before his teacher and asked: "Rav Aba, where is the wealth that was to come from Torah study?" Rav Aba said, "I see that he is not learning for the sake of heaven!" As he went to his room to consider what to do with Yosi, he heard a voice saying: "Do not punish him,

283. לְיוֹמִין, הֲוָה קָאִים קַמֵּיהּ, אָמַר לוֹ ר, אָן הוּא עוֹתְרָא. אָמַר שְׁמַע מִינָּה, דְּלָא לְשֵׁם שָׁמַיִם קָא עֲבִיד, וְעָאל לְאַדְרֵיהּ, שְׁמַע חַד קָלָא דַּהֲוָה אָמַר, לָא תַעֲנָשֵׁיהּ, דְּגַבְרָא רַבָּא לֶיהֱוֵי.

because he shall become a great man!" Rav Aba returned to Yosi and said: "Sit down, my son, sit down. I shall give you wealth."

תָּב לְגַבֵּיהּ, אֲמַר לֵיהּ, תִּיב בְּרִי תִּיב, וַאֲנָא יָהֵיבְנָא לָךְ עוּתְרָא.

At that moment a visitor appeared with a vessel made of pure gold. As he displayed it, its sparkle lit up the whole house. He said, "Rav, I wish to merit the understanding of Torah. But because I have not merited this understanding, I am searching for someone who can learn Torah for my sake. I inherited great wealth from my father, who used to set upon his table thirteen of these cups made of pure gold. I wish to achieve the merit of studying Torah, and I shall give my wealth to whomever achieves it for my sake."

284. אַדְהָכֵי, אָתָא גַּבְרָא וַזַד, וּמָאנָא דְּפָּז בִּידֵיהּ, אַפְּקֵיהּ וּנְפַל נְהוֹרָא בְּבֵיתָא. אָמַר לוֹ רַבִּי בָּעֵינָא לְמִזְכֵּי בְּאוֹרַיְיתָא, וַאֲנָא לָא זָכֵינָא, וּבָעֵינָא מָאן דְּיִשְׁתַּדַּל בְּאוֹרַיְיתָא בְּגִינִי. דְּהָא אִית לִי עוּתְרָא סַגִּי, דְּקָא שָׁבַק לִי אַבָּא, דְּכַד יָתֵיב עַל פָּתוֹרֵיהּ, הֲוָה מְסַדֵּר עֲלֵיהּ, תְּלֵיסַר כַּסֵּי מֵאלֵּין. וּבָעֵינָא לְמִזְכֵּי בְּאוֹרַיְיתָא, וַאֲנָא יָהֵיבְנָא עוּתְרָא.

Then Rav Aba said to Yosi the bachelor: "Study Torah, and this man will give you wealth!" The visitor then gave Rav Aba a cup of gold, and in response Rav Aba spoke the verse: "Gold and crystal cannot equal it. And

285. אָמַר לוֹ לְהַהוּא רַוָוק, תִּשְׁתַּדַּל בְּאוֹרַיְיתָא, וְדָא יָהֵיב לָךְ עוּתְרָא, יְהַב לֵיהּ הַהוּא כַּסָּא דְּפָז. קָרָא עֲלֵיהּ ר' אַבָּא, לֹא יַעַרְכֶנָּה זָהָב וּזְכוֹכִית וּתְמוּרָתָהּ כְּלִי פָז.

the exchange of it shall not be for vessels of fine gold." Yosi the bachelor then sat down and studied Torah, and the visitor gave him gold.

יָתִיב וְלָעָא בְּאוֹרַיְיתָא, וְהַהוּא בַּר נָשׁ הֲוָה יָהִיב לֵיהּ עוֹתְרָא.

As days passed, sincere desire for the Torah entered Yosi's heart. One day he sat down and wept. Rav Aba found him weeping and said: "Why are you weeping?" Yosi replied, "For the sake of this wealth, I am leaving behind the life in the World to Come! I do not want to learn anymore for the sake of this visitor, but rather to merit Torah for myself." Rav Aba said, "Now I see that Yosi is studying for the sake of heaven."

286. לְיוֹמִין עָאל וְחֲמִידוּ דְאוֹרַיְיתָא בִּמְעוֹי, יוֹמָא חַד הֲוָה יָתִיב, וַהֲוָה בָּכֵי. אַשְׁכְּחֵיהּ רַבֵּיהּ דַּהֲוָה בָּכֵי. אָמַר לוֹ עַל מָה קָא בָּכִית. אָמַר לוֹ, וּמָה מְנַּוְונָא וַחֲיֵי דְעָלְמָא דְאָתֵי, בְּגִין הַאי, לָא בְּעֵינָא אֶלָּא לְמִזְכֵּי לְגַבָּאי. אָמַר לוֹ הַשְׁתָּא ע"מ דְהָא לְשֵׁם שָׁמַיִם קָא עָבִיד.

Rav Aba called for the visitor and said to him: "Take your wealth back and share it with the poor and the orphans. I shall give you a bigger portion in the Torah, from all that we are learning!" Rav Yosi returned the gold that the visitor had given to him, and to this very day, the name "Son of Gold" (Heb. ben Pazi) has not been taken away from Rav Yosi or from his children.

287. קָרָא לֵיהּ לְהַהוּא גַּבְרָא, אָמַר לוֹ טוֹל עוֹתְרָךְ וְהַב לֵיהּ לְיַתְמֵי וּלְמִסְכְּנֵי, וַאֲנָא יְהִיבְנָא לָךְ וְחוּלַק יַתִּיר בְּאוֹרַיְיתָא, בְּכָל מַה דַאֲנָן לָעָאן. אַהֲדָר לֵיהּ ר' יוֹסֵי הַהוּא כַּסָּא דִּפָז, וְעַד יוֹמָא לָא אַעֲדֵי שְׁמֵיהּ וּמָן בְּנוֹי בֶּן פָּזִי, וְהַיְינוּ ר' יוֹסֵי בֶּן פָּזִי, וְזָכָה לְכַמָּה אוֹרַיְיתָא, הוּא וּבְנוֹי.

He became the famous Rav Yosi ben Pazi. He and his sons merited abundant Torah study, because there is no greater reward in the world than to study Torah. And payment for this study is not necessary, as it is written: "Gold and crystal cannot equal it; and the exchange of it shall not be for vessels of fine gold."

דְּלֵית לָךְ אֲגַר טַב בְּעָלְמָא כְּמַאן דְּלָעֵי בְּאוֹרַיְיתָא.

MEDITATION

If you find yourself becoming too involved with physical things, this meditation will help you regain your focus. Use it to strengthen your understanding that ultimate fulfillment comes from spiritual understanding and work.

דְּלֵית לָךְ אֲגַר טַב בְּעָלְמָא כְּמָאן

kema'an be'alma tav agar lach deleit

דְּלָעֵי בְּאוֹרַיְיתָא.

be'arayta dela'ei

There is no greater reward in the world than to study Torah. And payment for this study is not necessary, as it is written, "Gold and crystal cannot equal it; and the exchange of it shall not be for vessels of fine gold."

BECOMING BALANCED:

"THE FOREWORD TO THE IDRA RABA"

(ZOHAR, IDRA RABA, VERSE 8)

Most of the time, external influences dominate our lives. Someone or something upsets us, and we become focused on that feeling. But the kabbalists teach that maintaining a connection to the Light requires a stable spirit. This means remaining balanced regardless of what is said or heard or done.

This section of the Zohar concerns the importance of speech, and also of keeping silent. A constant need to talk, to show everyone the secrets we know, is a sign of an unstable spirit. Creating inner stability means training ourselves not to speak or react in impulsive ways. One must strive more and more toward getting a stable spirit.

Rav Shimon then opened the discussion saying: "'One who goes to tell tales reveals secrets. But he that is of a faithful spirit conceals the matter.' This verse is difficult. It should have said a 'man who tells tales' rather than a 'man who goes and tells tales.' What is a 'tale-goer?' This refers to someone who is not settled in his mind, and therefore is not trustworthy. Whatever he has heard goes within him like a board submerged in water that does not sink, and that shoots upward when it has been released. Which means: he cannot rest until he reveals whatever he heard to someone else. This is because the spirit of the one who tells tales is not settled and not stable. Of him who has a stable spirit, it is said: 'But he that is of a faithful spirit conceals the matter.' A faithful spirit means a stable spirit. Everything depends on spirit. It is also written: 'Do not let your mouth cause your flesh to sin.'"

8. ר"ש פָּתַח וְאָמַר, הוֹלֵךְ רָכִיל מְגַלֶּה סוֹד וְנֶאֱמַן רוּחַ מְכַסֶּה דָבָר. הוֹלֵךְ רָכִיל, הַאי קְרָא קַשְׁיָא, אִישׁ רָכִיל מִבָּעֵי לֵיהּ לְמֵימַר, מַאן הוֹלֵךְ. אֶלָּא מַאן דְּלָא אִתְיַישַׁב בְּרוּחֵיהּ, וְלָא הֲוֵי מְהֵימָנָא, הַהוּא מִלָּה דִּשְׁמַע, אָזִיל בְּגַוֵּיהּ כְּחֵיזְרָא בְּמַיָּא, עַד דִּרְמֵי לֵיהּ לְבַר. מ"ט. מִשּׁוּם דְּלֵית רוּחֵיהּ רוּחָא דְקִיּוּמָא. אֲבָל מַאן דְּרוּחֵיהּ רוּחָא דְקִיּוּמָא, בֵּיהּ כְּתִיב, וְנֶאֱמַן רוּחַ מְכַסֶּה דָבָר. וְנֶאֱמַן רוּחַ, קַיְימָא דְרוּחָא. בְּרוּחָא תַּלְיָא מִלְתָא. וּכְתִיב, אַל תִּתֵּן אֶת פִּיךָ לַחֲטִיא אֶת בְּשָׂרֶךָ.

181

MEDITATION

By reading this section, we awaken understanding of our need to develop a stable spirit, and we gain the assistance to do so.

אֲבָל מַאן דְּרוּחֵיהּ רוּחָא דְקִיּוּמָא, בֵּיהּ
beih dekiyuma rucha derucheih ma'an aval

כְּתִיב, וְנֶאֱמָן רוּחַ מְכַסֶּה דָבָר.
davar mechaseh ru'ach vene'eman ketiv

וְנֶאֱמָן רוּחַ, קִיּוּמָא דְּרוּחָא.
derucha kiyuna ru'ach vene'eman

Of him who has a stable spirit, it is said, 'But he that is of a faithful spirit conceals the matter.' A faithful spirit means a stable spirit.

UNDERSTANDING
THE GREATER REALITY:
"REMOVING THE FEAR OF DEATH"
(ZOHAR, VAYECHI, VERSE 744)

Living in this world, we think it is all there is. But an infinite spiritual realm also exists. One of the goals of our work is to stop living merely in the physical dimension and to develop awareness of the greater reality, as well as our place in it. The pain we experience in our daily lives comes from the narrowness of our focus. When we gain an awareness of the greater reality, pain and fear vanish.

This is also true of our fear of death. We fear death because it is a realm we are not aware of. But in this section, the Zohar explains that once we gain consciousness of the larger dimension, we can live in the infinite realm even before we pass on. Death becomes just a step from one realm into another, not an entrance into incomprehensible darkness. Here the Zohar discusses these ideas through the story of a father and his son. The son goes off to live and to grow, but the most joyful place is back when he returns to his father. Clearly, when we leave this world—provided we have achieved the spiritual growth and purpose for which we came—we return to a much better place.

The power of this section lies in breaking down the barriers between the physical and metaphysical worlds. We expand our consciousness beyond the physical dimension and open ourselves to the realms beyond.

If the souls are elevated on two sides—why then do they descend into this world, and why leave it? This is like a king who begot a son and sent him to be raised in a village, to be raised and taught the ways of the palace. When the king heard his son was grown up, out of love for him he sent the queen, his mother, to fetch him. She then brought him to the palace, where he rejoiced with his son every day.

744. וְאִי תֵימָא, הָא עִלָּאִין אִנּוּן מִתְּרֵין סִטְרִין, אַמַּאי נַחֲתִין לְהַאי עַלְמָא, וְאַמַּאי אִסְתַּלְקוּ מִנֵּיהּ. לְמַלְכָּא דְּאִתְיְלִיד לֵיהּ בַּר, שָׁדַר לֵיהּ לְוַוד כְּפַר, לְמַרְבְּיָה לֵיהּ, וּלְגַדְּלָא לֵיהּ, עַד דְּיִתְרַבֵּי, וְיוֹלְפּוּן לֵיהּ אָרְחֵי דְּהֵיכְלָא דְּמַלְכָּא. שָׁמַע מַלְכָּא, דְּהָא בְּרֵיהּ רַב וְאִתְרַבֵּי. מַה עֲבַד בִּרְחִימוּ דִּבְרֵיהּ, מְשַׁדַּר לָהּ לְמַטְרוֹנִיתָא אִמֵּיהּ בְּגִינֵיהּ, וְאָעִיל לְהֵיכְלֵיהּ, וְחָדֵי עִמֵּיהּ כָּל יוֹמָא.

The Creator also begot a son by the *Shechinah*. Who is the son? The Supernal Holy Soul. He sent him to the village—that is, to this world—to be raised and be brought up in the ways of the king's palace. When the king saw that his son was grown up in this village, and that it was time to bring him to the palace, what did he do? Out of love for his son, he sent the *Shechinah*, who brought him to the king's palace. The soul never leaves this world until the *Shechinah* comes for it and brings it to the king's palace, where it remains forever.

745. כָּךְ קוּדְשָׁא בְּרִיךְ הוּא, אוֹלִיד בַּר בְּמַטְרוֹנִיתָא, וּמַאי אִיהוּ נִשְׁמְתָא עִלָּאָה קַדִּישָׁא, שָׁדַר לֵיהּ לִכְפַר, לְהַאי עַלְמָא, דְּיִתְרַבֵּי בֵּיהּ, וְיוֹלְפּוּן לֵיהּ אוֹרְחֵי דְּהֵיכְלָא דְּמַלְכָּא. כֵּיוָן דְּיָדַע מַלְכָּא דְּהָא בְּרֵיהּ אִתְרַבֵּי בְּהַאי כְּפַר, וְעִידָן הוּא לְמַיְיתֵי לֵיהּ לְהֵיכְלֵיהּ. עֲבַד בִּרְחִימוּ דִּבְרֵיהּ, מְשַׁדַּר לְמַטְרוֹנִיתָא בְּגִינֵיהּ וְאָעִיל לֵיהּ לְהֵיכְלֵיהּ. נִשְׁמְתָא לָא סַלְקָא מֵהַאי עַלְמָא, עַד דְּאָתַת מַטְרוֹנִיתָא בְּגִינָהּ, וְאָעִילַת לָהּ בְּהֵיכְלָא דְּמַלְכָּא, וִיתִיבַת תַּמָּן לְעָלְמִין.

Yet it is the way of the world that the inhabitants of the village weep when the king's son parts from them. There was a wise man there in the village, who said: "Why are you crying? Is he not the king's son? It is not right that he should dwell among you any longer. He should dwell in his father's palace." Moses too, who was wise, saw the inhabitants of the village crying, and said to them: "You are the children of the Creator: you shall not gash yourselves."

Come and see, if all the righteous knew this, they would be glad when the day comes for them to depart from this world. For is it not a high honor that the *Shechinah* comes for them to escort them into the king's palace, and that the king will rejoice with them every day? For the Creator finds joy only with the souls of the righteous.

746. וְעִם כָּל דָּא, אוֹרְחָא דְעַלְמָא, דְּאִינּוּן בְּנֵי כְּפַר, בָּכָאן עַל פְּרִישׁוּ דִּבְרֵיהּ דְּמַלְכָּא מִנַּיְיהוּ. וַזד פִּקְחָא הֲוָה תַּמָּן, אֲמַר לוֹן עַל מָה מָה אַתּוּן בָּכָאן, וְכִי לָאו בְּרֵיהּ דְּמַלְכָּא אִיהוּ, וְלָא אִתְחֲזֵי לְמֶידַר יַתִּיר בֵּינַיְיכוּ, אֶלָּא בְּהֵיכָלָא דַּאֲבוֹי. כָּךְ מֹשֶׁה, דַּהֲוָה פִּקְחָ, וְחָמָא בְּנֵי כְּפַר דַּהֲוָה בָּכָאן. עַל דָּא אֲמַר, בָּנִים אַתֶּם לַיְיָ אֱלֹהֵיכֶם לֹא תִתְגֹּדְדוּ.

747. תָּא וְחֲזֵי, אִילּוּ הֲווֹ יָדְעִין כֻּלְּהוּ צַדִּיקַיָּיא הַאי, הֲווֹ וָזְדָאן הַהוּא יוֹמָא דְּמָטֵי לוֹן לְאִסְתַּלְּקָא מֵהַאי עָלְמָא, וְכִי לָאו יְקָרָא עִלָּאָה הוּא, דְּמַטְרוֹנִיתָא אָתַת בְּגִינַיְיהוּ, וּלְאוֹבְלָא לוֹן לְהֵיכָלָא לְמַלְכָּא, לְמֶחֱדֵי בְּהוּ מַלְכָּא כָּל יוֹמָא, דְּהָא קוּדְשָׁא בְּרִיךְ הוּא לָא אִשְׁתַּעֲשַׁע אֶלָּא בְּנִשְׁמָתְהוֹן דְּצַדִּיקַיָּא.

185

MEDITATION

With this meditation, we awaken our consciousness to a greater reality, within which there is no fear of death.

תָּא וַחֲזֵי, אִילוּ הֲווֹ יָדְעִין כֻּלְּהוּ צַדִּיקַיָּיא
tzadikaya kulhu yadin havu ilu chazei ta

הַאי, הֲווֹ וָדְאָן הַהוּא יוֹמָא דְּמָטֵי לוֹן
lon dematei yoma hahu chadan havo hai

לְאִסְתַּלְּקָא מֵהַאי עָלְמָא
alma meha'i le'istalka

Come and see, if all the righteous knew this, they would be glad when the day comes for them to depart from this world.

186

SPIRITUAL TEACHERS

AND FRIENDS:

"WHOSE HEART IS AWAKENED"

(ZOHAR, TRUMAH, VERSE 38)

When you find yourself struggling, look carefully at the people you've brought into your life. You can't sustain positive consciousness when you're surrounded by individuals whose consciousness is more negative than your own. Conversely, being in the presence of a righteous teacher or a friend whose consciousness is stronger than yours will strengthen your connection to the Light.

This doesn't mean you should immediately sever your connection with everyone whose spiritual work is not yet complete. On the contrary, you should even seek those people out. But it's essential to be aware of the roles people are playing in your life. Don't confuse those whom you can help with those who can teach and assist you.

The Zohar emphasizes *desire* for the Light as the most important quality to look for in a spiritual teacher. Learning and intellect are not the hallmarks of a great teacher. What's really essential is the teacher's desire for connection with the Light with all his heart and soul. The Zohar also emphasizes the importance of being in the presence of a teacher at all times, regardless of the difficulties that might be involved. In the section below, difficulty is what's meant by "pay in full." This is also an important assessment of our own growth. The Zohar states clearly that we can know if the Creator desires us by assessing our own inner desire for the Creator.

It is written: "They should bring Me an offering from every man whose heart is awakened..." That is, whoever overcomes his negative inclination is called 'man.' And what does "whose heart is awakened" mean? This means that God desires him, as it is written: "Of You my heart has said;" "the strength of my heart;" "of a merry heart;" and "His heart was merry." These all refer to the heart (the desire) of God. Here also, "Whose heart awakens him" refers to the desire of God. From him "you should take My offering," because that is where God is found. For God dwells in him and in no other place.

How do we know that God desires him and dwells in him? When we see that a person's intention is to pursue the Holy One, blessed be He, with his heart and soul, and desire. We are certain then that the spirit of God dwells in that person. Then we should pay in full (do whatever is necessary) to befriend him and to learn from him. About this, the

38. וְעַל דָּא כְּתִיב, וְיִקְחוּ לִי תְּרוּמָה מֵאֵת כָּל אִישׁ, מֵהַהוּא דְּאִקְרֵי אִישׁ, דְּאִתְגְּבַּר עַל יִצְרֵיהּ. וְכָל מַאן דְּאִתְגְּבַּר עַל יִצְרֵיהּ, אִקְרֵי אִישׁ. אֲשֶׁר יִדְּבֶנּוּ לִבּוֹ, מַאי אֲשֶׁר יִדְּבֶנּוּ לִבּוֹ. אֶלָּא. דְּיִתְרְעֵי בֵּיהּ קוּדְשָׁא בְּרִיךְ הוּא, כד'א לְךָ אָמַר לִבִּי. צוּר לְבָבִי. וְטוֹב לֵב. וַיִּיטַב לִבּוֹ. כֻּלְּהוּ בְּקוּדְשָׁא בְּרִיךְ הוּא קָאֲמַר. אוּף הָכָא אֲשֶׁר יִדְּבֶנּוּ לִבּוֹ. מִנֵּיהּ תִּקְחוּ אֶת תְּרוּמָתִי, דְּהָא תַּמָּן אִשְׁתְּכַח וְלָאו בַּאֲתַר אַחֲרָא.

39. וּמְנָא יַדְעִינָן דְּהָא קוּדְשָׁא בְּרִיךְ הוּא אִתְרְעֵי בֵּיהּ, וְשַׁוֵּי מְדוֹרֵיהּ בֵּיהּ. כַּד וַזְמֵינָן דִּרְעוּתָא דְּהַהוּא בַּר נָשׁ, לְמִרְדַּף וּלְאִשְׁתַּדְּלָא אֲבַתְרֵיהּ דִּקוּדְשָׁא בְּרִיךְ הוּא בְּלִבֵּיהּ וּבְנַפְשֵׁיהּ וּבִרְעוּתֵיהּ, וַדַּאי תַּמָּן יַדְעִינָן דְּשַׁרְיָא בֵּיהּ שְׁכִינְתָּא.

ancients said: "'...and acquire for yourself a friend.' You must buy him for a full price in order to merit the spirit of God that dwells in him. This is how far it is necessary to pursue a righteous man and earn him."

כְּדֵין בָּעֵינָן לְמִקְנֵי הַהוּא בַּר נָשׁ, בְּכֶסֶף שְׁלִים, לְאִתְחַבְּרָא בַּהֲדֵיהּ וּלְמֵילַף מִנֵּיהּ. וְעַל דָּא קַדְמָאֵי הֲווֹ אַמְרֵי, וּקְנֵה לְךָ חַבֵר, בְּאַגַּר שְׁלִים בָּעֵי לְמִקְנֵי לֵיהּ, בְּגִין לְמִזְכֵּי בִּשְׁכִינְתָּא. עַד הָכָא בָּעֵי לְמִרְדַּף בָּתַר זַכָּאָה וּלְמִקְנֵה לֵיהּ.

MEDITATION

This meditation ignites desire for closeness with spiritual teachers and friends. It strengthens your power to bring them into your life and kindles true appreciation for their presence.

וּמְנָא יַדְעִינָן דְּהָא קוּדְשָׁא בְּרִיךְ הוּא
umna   yadeinan   deha   kudsha   berich   hu

אִתְרְעֵי בֵּיהּ, וְשַׁוֵּי מָדוֹרֵיהּ בֵּיהּ. כַּד
itrei   beih   veshavei   madoreih   beih.   kad

וְזַמִּינָן דִּרְעוּתָא דְּהַהוּא בַּר נָשׁ, לְמִרְדַּף
chameinan   diruta   dehahu   bar   nash   lemirdaf

וּלְאִשְׁתַּדְלָא אֲבַתְרֵיהּ דְּקוּדְשָׁא בְּרִיךְ הוּא בְּלִבֵּיהּ
ule'ishtadla   avatrei   dekudsha   berich   hu   belibeih

וּבְנַפְשֵׁיהּ וּבִרְעוּתֵיהּ, וַדַּאי תַּמָּן יַדְעִינָן
uvenafsheih   uviru'eih   vadai   taman   yadinan

דְּשַׁרְיָא בֵּיהּ שְׁכִינְתָּא. כְּדֵין בְּעֵינָן
desharya   beih   shechinta.   kedein   ba'einan

לְמִקְנֵי הַהוּא בַּר נָשׁ, בְּכֶסֶף שְׁלִים
lemiknei   hahu   bar   nash,   bechesef   shelim

לְאִתְחַבְּרָא בַּהֲדֵיהּ וּלְמֵילַף מִנֵּיהּ
le'itchavra   bahadei   ulmeilaf   mineih

How do we know that God desires him and dwells in him? When we see that a person's intention is to pursue the Holy One, blessed be He, with his heart and soul and desire, we are certain then that the spirit of God dwells in that person. Then we should pay in full (do whatever is necessary) to befriend him and to learn from him.

The Battle:

"The Opponent is attacking"

(Zohar, Idra Raba, verse 1)

The great kabbalists compare spiritual work to a battle. If you think you've won the battle, you have already lost it. We need to remember this when we begin to take our spiritual life easily.

Kabbalistic study and meditation is not just relaxation. There is a constant struggle in the world between Light and darkness. The more Light that is present in the world, the more joy and fulfillment there is also; but more darkness means more pain and suffering. The Zohar teaches us to recognize this as a battle. Study is not just about gaining information. It is a means of revealing Light and removing darkness, thereby removing pain and suffering. In this section, in what is called the Great Assembly, Rav Shimon begins to reveal secrets (that is, Light) that have never been revealed before. He begins with a dramatic call to battle, to prepare his own consciousness and that of his students for the true spiritual purpose of their work.

The Zohar speaks about the need for living with three columns. Simply put, this concerns the concept of sharing: Right Column is Desire to Share, Left Column is Desire to Receive, and Central Column is restricting the Desire to Receive in favor of the Desire to Share. The Zohar says that only when we live with all three columns—not only sharing, and not only receiving—can Light truly be revealed.

We were taught that Rav Shimon said to his friends: "How long will we remain upheld by one pillar? It is written: 'It is time to take action for God: they have made void Your Torah.' The days are few and the Opponent is attacking. Every day the call resounds for repentance, and the reapers of the field are few. Those who understand the call are at the end of the vineyard, and even they do not heed the call.

1. תָּנֵא, אָמַר ר"ע לְוַזבְרַיָּיא, עַד אֵימַת נֵיתִיב בְּקַיְּימָא דְוַזד סַמְכָא. כְּתִיב עֵת לַעֲשׂוֹת לַיְיָ הֵפֵרוּ תוֹרָתֶךָ. יוֹמִין זְעֵירִין, וּמָארֵי דְוזוֹבָא דְוֹזִיק. כָּרוֹזָא קָארֵי כָּל יוֹמָא, וּמְוַזצְדֵי וַזקְלָא זְעֵירִין אִנּוּן. וְאִינְהוּ בְּשׁוּלֵי כַרְמָא. לָא אַשְׁגְּוזִן, וְלָא יַדְעִין, לְאָן אַתָר אָזְלִין כְּמָה דְיָאוֹת.

"Gather to the Throne, friends, with shields and swords and lances in your hands, Hurry with your repentance, your counsel, your wisdom, your understanding, your knowledge, your appearance, your hands, and your feet. Appoint as your King the one who has the authority of life and death, to decree truthful words to which the Supernal Holy One will listen, and will be glad to hear and to know."

2. אִתְכְּנָשׁוּ וַזבְרַיָּיא לְבֵי אִדְרָא, מְלוּבְּשִׁין שַׁרְיָין סַיְיפֵי וְרוּמְוזֵי בִּידֵיכוֹן, אִזְדְרְזוּ בְּתִקּוּנֵיכוֹן. בְּעֵיטָא, בְּוָזכְמְתָא. בְּסוּכְלְתָנוּ. בְּדַעְתָּא. בְּוֵזיזוּ. בִּידִין. בְּרַגְלִין. אַמְלִכוּ עֲלֵיכוֹן לְמַאן דִּבִרְשׁוּתֵיהּ וַזיֵי וּמוֹתָא. לְמִגְזַר מִלִּין דִּקְשׁוֹט. מִלִּין דְּקַדִּישֵׁי עֶלְיוֹנִין צַיְיתֵי לְהוּ, וְוַזדָאן לְמִשְׁמַע לְהוּ, וּלְמִנְדַּע לְהוּ.

Rav Shimon sat down and wept. He said, "Woe if I do reveal and woe if I do not reveal." The friends who were

3. יָתִיב ר"ע וּבָכָה, וְאָמַר וַוי אִי גָלֵינָא, וַוי אִי לָא גָלֵינָא. וַזבְרַיָּיא דַּהֲוָה תַּמָּן אִשְׁתִּיקוּ.

gathered there kept silent.
Finally, Rav Aba arose and
said to Rav Shimon: "If it is
right for my Master to
reveal, behold it is written,
'The secret of God is with
them that fear Him.' Your
friends fear the Holy One,
blessed be He. They had
already entered into the
previous assembly, where
you revealed secrets. Some of
them entered here, and some
of them exited."

We have learned that the
following friends were present:
Rav Elazar, Rav Shimon's
son; Rav Aba; Rav Yehuda;
Rav Yosi bar Yaakov; Rav
Yitzchak; Rav Chizkiyah bar
Rav; Rav Chiya; Rav Yosi;
and Rav Yesa. They reached
out to Rav Shimon with their
fingers pointed upward. They
entered the field among the
trees and sat down. Rav
Shimon stood and prayed
his prayer. Then he sat down
among the friends and said:
"Everyone should place his
hands in his bosom." Each
of the friends did so, and
Rav Shimon accepted them.

קָם ר' אַבָּא וא'כל, אִי נִיחָא
קַמֵּיהּ דְּמַר לְגַלָּאָה, הָא כְּתִיב
סוֹד יְיָ לִירֵאָיו, וְהָא וַחֲבְרַיָּיא
אִלֵּין דַּחֲלִין דְּקוּדְשָׁא בְּרִיךְ
הוּא אִינּוּן, וּכְבַר עָאלוּ
בְּאִדְרָא דְּבֵי מַשְׁכְּנָא, מִנְּהוֹן
עָאלוּ, מִנְּהוֹן נַפְקוּ.

4. תָּאנָא, אִתְמְנוֹ וַחֲבְרַיָּיא
קַמֵּיהּ דר'ש, וְאִשְׁתְּכָחוּ, רִבִּי
אֶלְעָזָר בְּרֵיהּ. ור' אַבָּא. ור'
יְהוּדָה. וְרִבִּי יוֹסֵי בַּר יַעֲקֹב.
ור' יִצְחָק. ור' חִזְקִיָּה בַּר רַב.
ור' חִיָּיא. ור' יוֹסֵי. ור' יֵיסָא.
יְדִין יָהֲבוּ לר'ש, וְאֶצְבְּעָן זַקְפוּ
לְעֵילָּא. וְעָאלוּ בְּחַקְלָא בֵּינֵי
אִילָנֵי וְיָתְבוּ. קָם ר'ש וְצַלֵּי
צְלוֹתֵיהּ, יָתִיב בְּגַוַויְיהוּ וְאָמַר,
כָּל חַד יְשַׁוֵּי יְדוֹי בְּתוּקְפֵּיהּ.
שַׁווּ יְדַיְיהוּ, וְנָסִיב לוֹן. פָּתַח
וְאָמַר אָרוּר הָאִישׁ אֲשֶׁר יַעֲשֶׂה
פֶסֶל וּמַסֵּכָה מַעֲשֵׂה יְדֵי וְזָרֵע
וְשָׂם בַּסָּתֶר וְעָנוּ כָּל הָעָם
וְאָמְרוּ אָמֵן.

He said, "Cursed be the man that makes any carved or molten idol, an abomination of God, the work of the hands of a craftsman, and sets it up in secret. And all the people shall answer and say: 'Amen.'"

Rav Shimon then said, "It is time to act for God. Why is this a time to act? Because 'they have made void Your Torah.' They have made void the Torah above, because she becomes void if she is not made in her perfection below. Of the Ancient of Days it is said, 'Happy are you, Israel; who is like you?' And it also says, 'Who is like You, God, among the gods?'"

5. פָּתַח ר'ש וְאָמַר, עֵת לַעֲשׂוֹת לַיְיָ, אֲמַאי עֵת לַעֲשׂוֹת לַיְיָ. מִשּׁוּם דְּהֵפֵרוּ תּוֹרָתֶךָ. מַאי הֵפֵרוּ תּוֹרָתֶךָ, תּוֹרָה דִּלְעֵילָא. דְּאִיהִי מִתְבַּטְּלָא אִי לָא יִתְעֲבִיד בְּתִקּוּנוֹי דָּא. וּלְעַתִּיק יוֹמִין אִתְּמַר. כְּתִיב אַשְׁרֶיךָ יִשְׂרָאֵל מִי כָמוֹךָ. וּכְתִיב, מִי כָמֹכָה בָּאֵלִים יְיָ.

Rav Shimon called on his son Rav Elazar, who sat in front of him. Rav Aba was on the other side and said: "Until now the three pillars were being constructed. But now we who are here together include all the spiritual elements." Then they were silent, until they heard a sound that made them

6. קָרָא לְרִבִּי אֶלְעָזָר בְּרֵיהּ, אוֹתְבֵיהּ קַמֵּיהּ, וּלְרִבִּי אַבָּא מִסִּטְרָא אַחֲרָא, וְאָמַר אֲנַן כְּלָלָא דְּכוֹלָא. עַד הַשָּׁתָא אִתְתַּקְנוּ קַיְימִין. אִשְׁתְּתִיקוּ, שַׁמְעֵי קָלָא, וְאַרְכּוּבָתָן דָּא לְדָא נַקְשָׁן. מַאי קָלָא. קָלָא דִּכְנוּפְיָיא עִלָּאָה דְּמִתְכַּנְּפֵי.

195

tremble. It was the sound of the friends who had died gathering in the Upper World.

Rav Shimon rejoiced and said: "God, I have heard of You, and I was afraid." It was true he feared, since at that moment he was connected with Chavakuk, who was of the Left Column. But for us who are united with the Central Column, our connection is based on love. It is written: "And you shall love God your Creator." It is also written: "Because God loved you" and it is also written: "I have loved you..."

7. וַדַּאי ר'ש וְאָמַר, יְיָ שָׁמַעְתִּי שִׁמְעֲךָ יָרֵאתִי הָתָם יָאוּת הֲוָה לְמֶחֱוֵי דָחִיל. אֲנָן בַּחֲבִיבוּתָא תַּלְיָיא מִלְתָא, דִּכְתִיב וְאָהַבְתָּ אֶת יְיָ אֱלֹהֶיךָ, וּכְתִיב מֵאַהֲבַת יְיָ אֶתְכֶם, וּכְתִיב אָהַבְתִּי אֶתְכֶם וְגוֹ.

MEDITATION

We've learned in other readings that we must never become complacent in our spiritual work. We must not forget that our work is a battle between Light and darkness. When we meditate on this section, we regain focus and clarity on the true battle that is ongoing in our lives.

אִתְכְּנִשׁוּ וַחֲבְרַיָּיא לְבֵי אַדְרָא, מְלוּבָּשִׁין שַׁרְיָין

sharyan melubashin idara lebei chavraya itkanashu

סַיָּיפֵי וְרוּמְחֵי בִּידֵיכוֹן, אִזְדְּרָזוּ בְּתִקּוּנֵיכוֹן.

betikuneichon iz'derazu bideichon verumchei sayifei

בְּעֵיטָא, בְּחָכְמְתָא. בְּסוּכְלְתָנוּ. בְּדַעְתָּא.

beda'eta besukletanu bechachmeta be'eita

בְּחֵיזוּ. בִּידִין. בְּרַגְלִין.

beraglin bidin becheizu

Gather to the Throne, friends, with shields and swords and lances in your hands, Hurry with your repentance, your counsel, your wisdom, your understanding, your knowledge, your appearance, your hands, and your feet.

HELPING OTHERS:

"PURSUE THOSE WHO HAVE NOT OVERCOME THEIR NEGATIVE INCLINATION"

(ZOHAR, TRUMAH, VERSE 40)

Sometimes we find friends in pain and in need of assistance but we don't know how to help them. While it's certainly important to assist with their immediate problem, we should also help them realize that the root cause of the situation is the absence of the Light. By awakening their connection to the Light, both the immediate problem and the root cause can be healed.

We might not even realize it, but the reason we're in this world is to help others in a lasting way. Moreover, we need to actively pursue those who need our help with the same energy that we seek those who can help us. Only by one person helping another—and then that person helping two more, and so on to infinity—can a critical mass be reached in which pain and suffering end once and for all.

As we saw in the previous section, more Light in the world means more joy and fulfillment; more darkness means more pain and suffering. So it is important now not only to bring about our own transformation, but also to assist others. You may doubt your ability to provide help, or that your own imperfections disqualify you from assisting others. You may find yourself thinking, "How can I help someone else, when I have so much chaos of my own?" But the Zohar strongly emphasizes that the blessings we draw into our lives manifest through the work of helping others to remove their darkness. This understanding, drawn from this section of the Zohar, is the basis of all The Kabbalah Centre's work.

The righteous should pursue those who have not overcome their negative inclination and purchase them for a full price in order to remove negativity from them, to subdue the Other Side in them, and to build them, for it is considered as though they had been newly created. This action elevates the greatness (Light) of God more than any other, and this elevation is higher than any other! What is the reason? Because through these actions the righteous caused the Other Side to be subdued and elevated the greatness of God, as it is written about Aaron: "And he turned many away from negative actions."

Come and see: Anyone who holds the hand of a person who has not overcome the negative inclination and endeavors to help him leave the path of negativity is elevated in three elevations, to which no other person can rise. He causes the subjugation of the Other Side, he causes the Creator to be elevated, and he causes the world to be preserved both

40. אוּף הָכִי, הַהוּא זַכָּאָה בָּעֵי לְמִרְדַּף בָּתַר וַזָּיִבָא, וּלְמִזְקְנֵי לֵיהּ בַּאֲגַר שָׁלִים, בְּגִין דְּיֵעֲבַר מִנֵּיהּ הַהוּא זוּהֲמָא, וְיִתְכַּפְיָא סִטְרָא אָחֳרָא, וְיַעֲבִיד לְנַפְשֵׁיהּ, בְּגִין דְּיִתְחֲוָשׁב עֲלֵיהּ, כְּאִילוּ הוּא בָּרָא לֵיהּ. וְדָא אִיהוּ שְׁבָחָא דְּיִסְתַּלַק בֵּיהּ יְקָרָא דְּקוּדְשָׁא בְּרִיךְ הוּא, יַתִּיר מִשְּׁבָחָא אָחֳרָא, וְאִסְתַּלְקוּתָא דָּא יַתִּיר מִכֹּלָּא. מַאי טַעֲמָא. בְּגִין דְּאִיהוּ גָּרִים לְאַכְפָּיָא סִטְרָא אָחֳרָא, וּלְאַסְתַּלְּקָא יְקָרָא דְּקוּדְשָׁא בְּרִיךְ הוּא. וְעַל דָּא כְּתִיב בְּאַהֲרֹן, וְרַבִּים הֵשִׁיב מֵעָוֹן. וּכְתִיב בְּרִיתִי הָיְתָה אִתּוֹ.

41. תָּא וַחֲזֵי, כָּל מַאן דְּאָחֵיד בִּידָא דְּחַיָּיבָא, וְאִשְׁתַּדַּל בֵּיהּ, לְמִשְׁבַּק אָרְחָא בִּישָׁא, אִיהוּ אִסְתַּלְּק בִּתְלַת סְלוּקִין, מַה דְּלָא אִסְתַּלְּק הָכִי בַּר נָשׁ אָחֳרָא. גָּרִים לְאַכְפָּיָיא סִטְרָא אָחֳרָא. וְגָרִים דְּאִסְתַּלְּק קוּדְשָׁא בְּרִיךְ הוּא בִּיקָרֵיהּ. וְגָרִים לְקַיְּימָא כָּל עָלְמָא בְּקִיּוּמֵיהּ לְעֵילָּא וְתַתָּא.

above and below. About this person, it is written: "My bond was with him for life and peace" and he merits to see the children of his children, and gains merit in this world and in the World to Come. All the accusers will not be able to judge him in this world and in the World to Come. He enters through the twelve gates, and there is nothing to prevent him from entering. It is written: "His seed shall be mighty upon earth; the generation of the upright shall be blessed. Wealth and riches shall be in his house, and his righteousness endures forever. Light rises in the darkness for the upright: he is gracious and full of compassion, and just..."

וְעַל הַאי בַּר נָשׁ כְּתִיב, בְּרִיתִי הָיְתָה אִתּוֹ הַחַיִּים וְהַשָּׁלוֹם. וְזָכֵי לְמֶחֱזֵי בְּנִין לִבְנוֹי, וְזָכֵי בְּהַאי עָלְמָא, וְזָכֵי לְעָלְמָא דְּאָתֵי. כָּל מָארֵי דִּינִין, לָא יַכְלִין לְמֵידָן לֵיהּ, בְּהַאי עָלְמָא וּבְעָלְמָא דְּאָתֵי. עָאל בִּתְרֵיסַר תַּרְעֵי, וְלֵית מַאן דִּימַחֵי בִּידֵיהּ. וְעַל דָּא כְּתִיב, גִּבּוֹר בָּאָרֶץ יִהְיֶה זַרְעוֹ דּוֹר יְשָׁרִים יְבֹרָךְ. הוֹן וָעֹשֶׁר בְּבֵיתוֹ וְצִדְקָתוֹ עוֹמֶדֶת לָעַד. זָרַח בַּחֹשֶׁךְ אוֹר לַיְשָׁרִים וְגוֹ'.

MEDITATION

This section brings appreciation of how important it is
to assist others and awakens your ability to take action
in assisting those who need your help.

תָּא חֲזֵי, כָּל מַאן דְּאָחִיד בִּידָא דְּחַיָּיבָא,
chazei ta kol ma'an de'achid bida dechayava

וְאִשְׁתָּדַּל לְמִשְׁבַּק אָרְחָא בִּישָׁא, אִיהוּ
ve'ishtada lemishvak beih archa bisha ihu

אִסְתַּלָּק בִּתְלַת סְלוּקִין, מַה דְּלָא אִסְתַּלָּק הָכִי
bitlat istalak silukin ma dela istalak hachi

בַּר נָשׁ אָחֳרָא.
bar nash achra

*Come and see: Anyone who holds the hand of a person who
has not overcome the negative inclination and endeavors to
help him leave the path of negativity is elevated in three
elevations, to which no other person can rise.*

Spreading the Zohar:

"When The Zohar will be revealed, multitudes will gather to it"

(Zohar, Chadash Tikkunim, verse 114A)

Here the Zohar compares its power to that of Noah's ark. During Noah's time there was destruction throughout the world, but those who entered the ark were protected. In the same way, we who enter the Zohar are protected from the darkness that exists in our own time. Moreover, the Zohar predicts that when the Zohar is at last revealed after so many centuries of concealment, multitudes of people will gather to connect with it. It is this gathering around the Zohar—like entering an ark—that will enable the world to fulfill its purpose.

Connecting to the Zohar is actually an experience of going back in time to the moment in history when a great revelation took place at the gathering of all the righteous souls. On a personal note, I believe that an important part of my work is making it possible for people to gather around the Zohar, to enter it, and to gain connection with its Light.

This book is like Noah's ark, into which gather all the different kinds and species. So too all the souls of the righteous and people of stature come together in this book. About them it is said, "This is the gate of God. The righteous come through it, and those who are not righteous do not enter."

When this composition of the Zohar will be revealed in the world, multitudes will gather to it. Of them it is said, "Those who are here today, and those that are not with us — through this composition they are all with us today."

וְהַאי וְחִבּוּרָא הוּא כְּגַוְונָא דְּתֵבַת נֹחַ דְּאִתְכְּנַשׁ בֵּיהּ כָּל מִין וָמִין, הָכִי מִתְכַּנְּשִׁין בְּהַאי וְחִבּוּרָא כָּל נִשְׁמָתִין דְּצַדִּיקַיָּא וְאַנְשֵׁי מִדּוֹת, דְּאִתְּמַר בְּהוֹן, זֶה הַשַּׁעַר לַיהֹוָ"ה צַדִּיקִים יָבֹאוּ בוֹ, וְאָחֳרָנִין דְּלָאו צַדִּיקִים אִתְדַּחְיָין מִתַּמָּן.

וְכַד אִתְגַּלְיָא הַאי וְחִבּוּרָא בְּעָלְמָא, סַגִּיאִין מִתְכַּנְּשִׁין לְגַבֵּיהּ, דְּאִתְּמַר בְּהוֹן, כִּי אֶת אֲשֶׁר יֶשְׁנוֹ פֹּה וְגוֹמֵר, וְאֵת אֲשֶׁר אֵינֶנּוּ פֹּה, בְּהַאי וְחִבּוּרָא עִמָּנוּ הַיּוֹם.

MEDITATION

By reading this section, we awaken the Zohar's Light of protection and the revelation of the Light of the Zohar in the world.

וְכַד   אִתְגַּלְיָא הַאי וְּבוּרָא בְּעָלְמָא,
be'alma chibura hai   itgalya vechad

סַגִּיאִין   מִתְכַּנְּשִׁין   לְגַבֵּיה
legabeih   mitkanshin   sagi'in

When this composition of the Zohar will be revealed in the world. Multitudes will gather to it.

Tree of Life:

"Because they will taste the Zohar"

(Zohar, Naso, verse 90)

In this reading, Moses is speaking to Rav Shimon bar Yochai. Moses explains that the wise—that is, those who study the Zohar—"shall shine like the firmament," which denotes their deep connection with the Light of the Creator, the source of our fulfillment, the true essence of the Zohar. This is the meaning of the several metaphors used in this passage, such as the Tree of Life, the *Sfirah* of *Binah*, and the Supernal Mother, which is called "repentance."

Moses states that all those who have connection with the Zohar will require no cleansing or test to connect with the final revelation and the coming of *Mashiach* (Messiah). When the Zohar uses this term, it refers to the time when all humanity will achieve fulfillment and the removal of all pain, suffering, and death—a time when there is a complete revelation of Light.

We should be aware that the term *Israelite* does not refer to a particular nation or ethnic group; it refers to those who engage in spiritual work and the study of the Zohar. When Moses speaks of a "taste from the Tree of Life," this refers to a complete connection with the Zohar in heart, mind, body, and soul—including even the sense of taste.

The closing sentence of this reading describes the total clarity that will exist at the time of the final revelation, when the presence of the Creator will be absolutely clear, and all chaos and confusion will end.

"But the wise shall understand," since they are from the side of *Binah*, which is the Tree of Life. For them, it was said: "'And they who are wise shall shine like the brightness (Zohar) of the firmament' with your composition, which is the book of the Zohar, from the Light of the Supernal Mother, called "repentance." They do not require a test or a purification: because the Israelites in the future will taste from the Tree of Life, which is this book of the Zohar. They will leave the exile with mercy. It will hold true about them that 'the Creator alone will lead them, and there will be no strange God with him.'"

‎90. וְהַמַּשְׂכִּלִים יָבִינּוּ, מִסִּטְרָא דְּבִינָה, דְּאִיהוּ אִילָנָא דְחַיֵּי, בְּגִינַיְיהוּ אִתְּמַר, וְהַמַּשְׂכִּלִים יַזְהִירוּ כְּזוֹהַר הָרָקִיעַ בְּהַאי חִבּוּרָא דִּילָךְ דְּאִיהוּ סֵפֶר הַזֹּהַר, מִן זוֹהֲרָא דְּאִימָא עִלָּאָה תְּשׁוּבָה. בְּאִלֵּין לָא צָרִיךְ נִסָּיוֹן, וּבְגִין דַּעֲתִידִין יִשְׂרָאֵל לְמִטְעַם מֵאִילָנָא דְחַיֵּי, דְּאִיהוּ הַאי סֵפֶר הַזֹּהַר, יִפְּקוּן בֵּיהּ מִן גָּלוּתָא בְּרַחֲמֵי. וְיִתְקַיַּים בְּהוֹן, יְיָ בָּדָד יַנְחֶנּוּ וְאֵין עִמּוֹ אֵל נֵכָר.

MEDITATION

With this meditation, we awaken our ability to taste
the Zohar with our whole being through our study.
Through the deep connection this study brings, we
move ourselves and the whole world closer to the end
of all pain, suffering, and even death.

וּבְגִין דַּעֲתִידִין יִשְׂרָאֵל לְמִטְעַם מֵאִילָנָא דְחַיֵּי,
dechayei meilana lemitam Israel da'atidin uvegin

דְּאִיהוּ הַאי סֵפֶר הַזֹּהַר, יִפְּקוּן בֵּיהּ מִן
min beih yifk'on haZohar sefer hai de'ihu

גָּלוּתָא בְּרַחֲמֵי.
berachamei galuta

And because the Israelites in the future will taste from the
Tree of Life, which is this book of the Zohar. They will leave
the exile with mercy.

IMMORTALITY:

"HE WILL SWALLOW UP DEATH FOREVER"

(ZOHAR, BERESHEET A, VERSE 481)

In this final section, the Zohar speaks of the perfected world, which is the ultimate purpose of Creation and the goal of our spiritual work. As the Zohar makes clear, through our work we can bring about a world in which pain, suffering, and even death itself are eliminated forever.

Rav Yitzchak said that all those generations, which originated with and came from Shet, were pious and righteous. Subsequently, as they spread and multiplied, they learned earthly skills of destruction with swords and spears, This continued until Noach came. When Noach first came, they did not sow and reap. He improved the world for them and taught them to cultivate the land, and they depended on agriculture. This is what is meant by the verse: "While the earth remains..."

481. אָמַר ר' יִצְחָק, כָּל דָּרִין דְּאִשְׁתַּכְלָלוּ מִשֵׁת, כֻּלְּהוּ צַדִּיקֵי וַוְסִידֵי לְבָתַר אִתְפַּשְׁטוּ וְאוֹלִידוּ וְאוֹלִיפוּ אוּמָנוּתָא דְּעָלְמָא, לְשֵׁיצָאָה בְּרוּמְחִין וּסַיְיפִין, עַד דְּאָתָא נֹחַ, וְאַתְקִין לוֹן תִּקּוּנָא דְּעָלְמָא, וּלְמִפְלַח וּלְאַתְקָנָא אַרְעָא, דְּהָא בְּקַדְמֵיתָא לָא הֲווֹ זָרְעִין וְזָוְזְדִין, לְבָתַר אִצְטְרִיכוּ לְהַאי. דִּכְתִיב עוֹד כָּל יְמֵי הָאָרֶץ וְגוֹ'.

Rav Elazar said that in the future, the Creator will correct the world and transform the spirit of life in people so that they live forever. About this, it is written: "For as the days of a tree shall the days of my people be," and "He will swallow up death forever; and the Creator will wipe away tears from off all faces; and the blemish of His people shall He take away from off all the earth: for the Creator has spoken it."

482. ר' אֶלְעָזָר אָמַר, זְמִין קָדוֹשׁ בָּרוּךְ הוּא לְתַקָּנָא עָלְמָא, וּלְאַתְקָנָא רוּחָא בִּבְנֵי נָשָׁא, בְּגִין דְּיוֹרְכוּן יוֹמִין לְעָלְמִין, הֲדָא הוּא דִכְתִיב, כִּי כִּימֵי הָעֵץ יְמֵי עַמִּי וְגוֹ'. וּכְתִיב וּבִלַּע הַמָּוֶת לָנֶצַח, וּמָחָה ה' אֱלֹקִים דִּמְעָה מֵעַל כָּל פָּנִים וְחֶרְפַּת עַמּוֹ יָסִיר מֵעַל כָּל הָאָרֶץ, כִּי ה' דִּבֵּר.

MEDITATION

Through the words of this meditation, we awaken ourselves in heart and mind to the true purpose of Creation. When we read this section, we also bring ourselves and the world one step closer to a world in which pain, suffering, and even death itself are eliminated forever.

ר׳ אֶלְעָזָר אָמַר, זַמִין קָדוֹשׁ בָּרוּךְ הוּא
hu baruch kadosh zamin amar Elazar Ribbi

לְתַקָנָא עָלְמָא, וּלְאַתְקָנָא רוּחָא בִּבְנֵי נְשָׁא,
nesha bivnei rucha ulatkana alma letakana

בְּגִין דְיוֹרְכוּן יוֹמִין לְעָלְמִין
le'almin yomin deyorchun begin

Rav Elazar said that in the future, the Creator will correct the world and transform the spirit of life in people so that they live forever.

THE ZOHAR

"Bringing *The Zohar* from near oblivion to wide accessibility has taken many decades. It is an achievement of which we are truly proud and grateful."

—Michael Berg

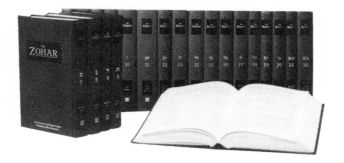

Composed more than 2,000 years ago, *The Zohar* is a set of 23 books, a commentary on biblical and spiritual matters in the form of conversations among spiritual masters. But to describe *The Zohar* only in physical terms is greatly misleading. In truth, *The Zohar* is nothing less than a powerful tool for achieving the most important purposes of our lives. It was given to all humankind by the Creator to bring us protection, to connect us with the Creator's Light, and ultimately to fulfill our birthright of true spiritual transformation.

More than eighty years ago, when The Kabbalah Centre was founded, *The Zohar* had virtually disappeared from the world. Few people in the general population had ever heard of it.

Whoever sought to read it—in any country, in any language, at any price—faced a long and futile search.

Today all this has changed. Through the work of The Kabbalah Centre and the editorial efforts of Michael Berg, *The Zohar* is now being brought to the world, not only in the original Aramaic language but also in English.

The new English *Zohar* provides everything for connecting to this sacred text on all levels: the original Aramaic text for scanning; an English translation; and clear, concise commentary for study and learning.

More products that can help you bring the wisdom of Kabbalah into your life

The Sacred Zohar
Deluxe *Aramaic* Edition

Here is the complete Zohar in its pure form—the original Aramaic—in a single volume of almost 2,000 pages. Designed to complement the 23-volume set of Aramaic with English Translation and Commentary, this handsome volume is printed on fine onion-skin paper, with gilded edges, and bound in deluxe, foil-stamped cover material, with a ribbon marker. *The Sacred Zohar* comes gift-boxed and includes a velvet pouch.

Becoming Like God
By Michael Berg

At the age of 16, kabbalistic scholar Michael Berg began the herculean task of translating *The Zohar*, Kabbalah's chief text, from its original Aramaic into its first complete English translation. *The Zohar*, which consists of 23 volumes, is considered a compendium of virtually all information pertaining to the universe, and its wisdom is only beginning to be verified today.

During the ten years he worked on *The Zohar*, Michael Berg discovered the long-lost secret for which humanity has searched for more than 5,000 years: how to achieve our ultimate destiny. *Becoming Like God* reveals the transformative method by which people can actually break free of what is called "ego nature" to achieve total joy and lasting life.

Berg puts forth the revolutionary idea that for the first time in history, an opportunity is being made available to humankind: an opportunity to Become Like God.

The Secret
By Michael Berg

Like a jewel that has been painstakingly cut and polished, *The Secret* reveals life's essence in its most concise and powerful form. Michael Berg begins by showing you how our everyday understanding of our purpose in the world is literally backwards. Whenever there is pain in our lives—indeed, whenever there is anything less than complete joy and fulfillment—this basic misunderstanding is the reason.

Well of Life
By Michael Berg

According to the teachings of Kabbalah, portions of the Bible or Torah connect to distinct weekly energies. Tapping into those energies helps to connect us with the Light, the source of all the positive energy we experience in life. In *Well of Life*, noted Kabbalistic scholar, editor, and author Michael Berg has given us an inspirational and useful guide, meant to be read throughout the year to increase the power and depth of our spiritual work and lead us on the path to a happier life.

Fifty-two short chapters, corresponding to each week of the lunar year, tell and decode key stories from the Bible, revealing the lessons to be learned from them. Although the readings are from Biblical sources, the wisdom is universal and not religious in tone. It simply provides helpful ways of thinking about life, one's purpose, and how to create a richer, more meaningful life experience.

The Living Kabbalah System™: Out of the Darkness™

Take Your Life to the Next Level™ with this step-by-step, 23-day system for transforming your life and achieving lasting fulfillment.

This revolutionary interactive system incorporates the latest learning strategies, addressing all three learning styles:

- Auditory (recorded audio sessions)

- Visual (workbook with written concepts and graphics)

- Tactile (written exercises, self-assessments, and physical tools)

The sturdy carrying case makes the system easy and convenient to use, in the car, at the gym, on a plane, wherever and whenever you choose. Learn from today's great Kabbalah leaders—Kabbalistic scholar Yehuda Berg and Instructor Jamie Greene—in an intimate, one-on-one learning atmosphere. You get practical, actionable tools and exercises to integrate the wisdom of Kabbalah into your daily life. In just 23 days you can learn to live with greater intensity, be more successful in business and relationships, and achieve your dreams. Why wait? Take your life to the next level starting today.

218

The Power of Kabbalah
By Yehuda Berg

 Imagine your life filled with unending joy, purpose, and contentment. Imagine your days infused with pure insight and energy. This is *The Power of Kabbalah*. It is the path from the momentary pleasure that most of us settle for, to the lasting fulfillment that is yours to claim. Your deepest desires are waiting to be realized. But they are not limited to the temporary rush from closing a business deal, the short-term high from drugs, or a passionate sexual relationship that lasts only a few short months.

Wouldn't you like to experience a lasting sense of wholeness and peace that is unshakable, no matter what may be happening around you? Complete fulfillment is the promise of Kabbalah. Within these pages, you will learn how to look at and navigate through life in a whole new way. You will understand your purpose and how to receive the abundant gifts waiting for you. By making a critical transformation from a reactive to a proactive being, you will increase your creative energy, get control of your life, and enjoy new spiritual levels of existence. Kabbalah's ancient teaching is rooted in the perfect union of the physical and spiritual laws already at work in your life. Get ready to experience this exciting realm of awareness, meaning, and joy.

The wonder and wisdom of Kabbalah has influenced the world's leading spiritual, philosophical, religious, and scientific minds. Until today, however, it was hidden away in ancient texts, available only to scholars who knew where to look. Now after many centuries, *The Power of Kabbalah* resides right here in this one remarkable book. Here, at long last is the complete and simple path—actions you can take right now to create the life you desire and deserve.

The 72 Names of God: Technology for the Soul™
By Yehuda Berg

The story of Moses and the Red Sea is well known to almost everyone; it's even been an Academy Award–winning film. What is not known, according to the internationally prominent author Yehuda Berg, is that a state-of-the-art technology is encoded and concealed within that biblical story. This technology is called the 72 Names of God, and it is the key—your key—to ridding yourself of depression, stress, creative stagnation, anger, illness, and other physical and emotional problems. In fact, the 72 Names of God is the oldest, most powerful tool known to mankind—far more powerful than any 21st century high-tech know-how when it comes to eliminating the garbage in your life so that you can wake up and enjoy life each day. Indeed, the 72 Names of God is the ultimate pill for anything and everything that ails you because it strikes at the DNA level of your soul.

The power of the 72 Names of God operates strictly on a soul level, not a physical one. It's about spirituality, not religiosity. Rather than being limited by the differences that divide people, the wisdom of the Names transcends humanity's age-old quarrels and belief systems to deal with the one common bond that unifies all people and nations: the human soul.

Wheels of a Soul
By Rav Berg

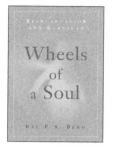

In *Wheels of a Soul,* Kabbalist Rav Berg reveals the keys to answering these and many more questions that lie at the heart of our existence as human beings. Specifically, Rav Berg explains why we must acknowledge and explore the lives we have already lived in order to understand the life we are living today . . .

Make no mistake: *you have been here before.* Reincarnation is a fact—and just as science is now beginning to recognize that time and space may be nothing but illusions, Rav Berg shows why death itself is the greatest illusion of all.

In this book you learn much more than the answers to these questions. You will understand your true purpose in the world and discover tools to identify your life's soul mate. Read *Wheels of a Soul* and let one of the greatest kabbalistic masters of our time change your life forever.

God Wears Lipstick
By Karen Berg

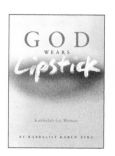

God Wears Lipstick is written exclusively for women (or for men who better want to understand women) by one of the driving forces behind the Kabbalah movement.

For thousands of years, women were banned from studying Kabbalah, the ancient source of wisdom that explains who we are and what our purpose is in this universe.

Karen Berg changed that. She opened the doors of The Kabbalah Centre to anyone who wanted to understand the wisdom of Kabbalah and brought Light to these people.

In *God Wears Lipstick*, Karen Berg shares that wisdom with us, especially as it affects you and your relationships. She reveals a woman's special place in the universe and why women have a spiritual advantage over men. She explains how to find your soulmate and your purpose in life. She empowers you to become a better human being as you connect to the Light, and she then gives you the tools for living and loving.

THE KABBALAH CENTRE

The International Leader in the Education of Kabbalah

Since its founding, The Kabbalah Centre has had a single mission: to improve and transform people's lives by bringing the power and wisdom of Kabbalah to all who wish to partake of it.

Through the lifelong efforts of Kabbalists Rav and Karen Berg, and the great spiritual lineage of which they are a part, an astonishing 3.5 million people around the world have already been touched by the powerful teachings of Kabbalah. And each year, the numbers are growing!

. . . .

If you were inspired by this book in any way and would like to know how you can continue to enrich your life through the wisdom of Kabbalah, here is what you can do next:

Call 1-800-KABBALAH where trained instructors are available 18 hours a day. These dedicated people are willing to answer any and all questions about Kabbalah and help guide you along in your effort to learn more.

On this journey, we are but halves of souls. While we may know the pain of the heart, the pain of our soul for the lack of the missing half is beyond both measure and human perception.

May the Light you reveal in the pages of this book open your heart and mine—wide enough to warrant the closeness of the soul mate for which we all long. And as the Kabbalists teach, as you pray for others, know for sure your own prayers will be answered first.